Steve Parish™

PUBLISHING

Amazing Facts about Australian

Birds

Principal Photographer: Steve Parish

Text: Karin Cox

AMAZING FACTS — AUSTRALIAN BIRDS

Contents

RON & VALERIE TAYLOR

Australia's
amazing birds

Earth's skies and shores are home to approximately 9800 bird species and about 850 of them occupy Australia and its island territories — about 760 of these are native to this continent. The power of flight has allowed these incredible animals to settle in almost every habitat on the planet, from the icy wasteland of Antarctica to the arid, stifling deserts.

AUSTRALIA'S BIRD SPECIES have been added to over time by arrivals from other continents; likewise, some of our native bird species have colonised nearby islands. Many species are descendants of the birds that diversified when Australia was still part of the ancient supercontinent known as Gondwana. When the landmass that is now Australia drifted away from Antarctica and New Zealand, it took with it plant and animal species that, over time, evolved in isolation to suit Australian environmental conditions.

In the past, Australia was much hotter and wetter than it is now. Gradually, as the continent drifted north, its climate changed and became drier. Some bird species remained in the relics of ancient rainforest; others become well adapted to deal with heat and drought. Some species, such as honeyeaters, formed special relationships with certain food plants that benefited both the plants and the birds.

Around 60,000 years ago, the arrival of humans also began to impact on the lifestyles of birds. Aborigines used fire as a way of clearing land and to encourage or discourage the growth of certain plants, many of which had dependent bird species. Since European settlement, the introduction of hoofed domestic stock and clearing for development and agriculture have also changed the face of the land. This has often been to the detriment of native species, although some birds, such as Emus, have benefited from the increase in dams and bores, which provide more readily available water in arid areas.

Anticlockwise from top left: Regent Bowerbird; Emu; Southern Cassowary; Aboriginal artwork depicting the Emu and Southern Cassowary; Male Australian King-Parrot.

Archaeopteryx
— earliest known bird

Some 150 million years ago, Archaeopteryx, *the first bird, appeared.* Archaeopteryx *was about the size of a modern chicken and also had some reptilian features, although it was* Archaeopteryx's *feathers and wishbone (like that of modern birds) that distinguished it as a bird. This early bird's fossilised form was found in 1861 preserved in fine-grained limestone in Solnhofen, Germany.*

Archaeopteryx lithographica

AT FIRST, SCIENTISTS WERE UNSURE about whether or not *Archaeopteryx* could fly. However, in 2004, studies conducted by palaeontologists at London's Natural History Museum and the University of Texas in the United States used computer imaging of *Archaeopteryx's* fossilised skull to discover that its brain was remarkably bird-like and was equipped with the neurosensory requirements for flight.

Following *Archaeopteryx* came several other examples of ancient bird, such as *Confuciusornis sanctus* and the flightless 1.7 m *Hesperornis* and *Ichthyornis*, which lived around 115 million years ago in the early Cretaceous Period. Around 100 million years ago, the first "modern" birds appeared. These were known as the Neornithes (the new birds) and they diversified into many groups.

There is a lot of debate over whether birds evolved from reptilian dinosaurs or vice versa, and even whether birds and dinosaurs evolved independently. Most scientists believe birds evolved from the reptilian archosaurs.

the FACTS!

MANY PEOPLE MISTAKENLY believe that Pterosaurs and Pterodactyls were the first birds. In fact these dinosaurs were reptiles.

FROM AN EVOLUTIONARY PERSPECTIVE, birds are younger than mammals, having appeared almost 100 million years later.

BIRDS PROBABLY EVOLVED from archosaurs, which were reptiles. Consequently, they share an important feature: egg-laying. However, birds are unlike reptiles in that they are endothermic (or warm-blooded), are feathered and incubate their eggs.

A FOSSIL FEATHER known as the Koonwarra feather (below) was found in South Gippsland, Victoria, in the 1980s. It probably came from a bird about the size of a Red-browed Finch, although it was 115–118 million years old and not from the modern Neornithes type.

MUSEUM OF VICTORIA

FOSSILS OF A GIANT PENGUIN, *Anthropornis nordenskjoeldi*, have been found south-west of Adelaide, South Australia. Scientists estimate it lived around 40–45 million years ago, weighed about 90 kg and stood to at least 1.35 m tall.

GIGANTIC RELATIVES

The largest feathered animal known to science was believed to be the prehistoric Stirton's Thunder Bird (*Dromornis stirtoni*). This large, duck-like bird lived more than 6 million years ago, stood 3 m high and probably weighed as much as 500 kg. However, a very recent discovery in China has possibly turned up an even larger feathered prehistoric animal. The 1400 kg and 5 m tall *Gigantoraptor erlianensis* was found in Mongolia's Erlian basin in 2005.

Although still classified as megafauna, the smaller *Genyornis newtoni* (right) also roamed Australia and weighed in at 44 kg. It is quite possible that early Indigenous Australians hunted *Genyornis*, which became extinct around 46,000 years ago, shortly after humans inhabited the continent.

What is a bird?

Birds belong to the class Aves and have two major distinguishing features that set them apart from all other animals — feathers and beaks. Taxonomy classifies all of the world's birds into groups based on their similarities and differences.

the FACTS!

FOSSIL EVIDENCE suggests that penguins, loons, grebes, pelicans and cormorants had a distinct evolutionary lineage separate from other bird species.

GRUIFORMES (rails and cranes) have one of the most comprehensive fossil records.

THE LARGEST ORDER is that of the passerines, which comprises about 5800 species.

THE FOSSIL RECORDS of birds in the order Procellariiformes, which include the tube-nosed petrels and albatrosses, go back around 60 million years.

THE SCALES ON A BIRD'S LEGS are reminiscent of their reptilian ancestry, although some cold-climate birds have evolved to have feathers on their legs and toes.

SCIENTISTS ARE NOW USING DNA to better understand relationships between modern bird species. All modern birds (or Neornithes) are divided into two groups — Paleognaths (or ancient jawed birds), which include the ratites (birds like the Emu or ostrich) and predate the break-up of Gondwana, and Neognaths (or new jawed birds), which have more advanced skull structures. Over 99% of all bird species alive today are Neognaths. The oldest modern birds are therefore the flightless ratites, which came into existence some 85 million years ago. Fossil records show that most of today's bird families were alive in the Eocene Epoch (57–37 million years ago) or Oligocene Epoch (37–24 million years ago), but some can be traced back to the early Cretaceous Period. The orders Galliformes (which include chickens, pheasants and quails) and Anseriforms (comprised of ducks and other waterfowl) have some of the more primitive lineages.

ORDERING & NAMING BIRDS

There are currently around 27 orders of birds, although some ornithologists recognise more. Birds grouped into each order have features that are unique to that order. For example, owls belong to the order Strigiformes, because all owls have a bony arch on the radius, as well as other similar features. Each order is divided into families (of which there are around 165), then genera (more than 2000) and then species. Each species is defined as being separate from other similar animals in the same genus because of differences that make interbreeding unlikely between them.

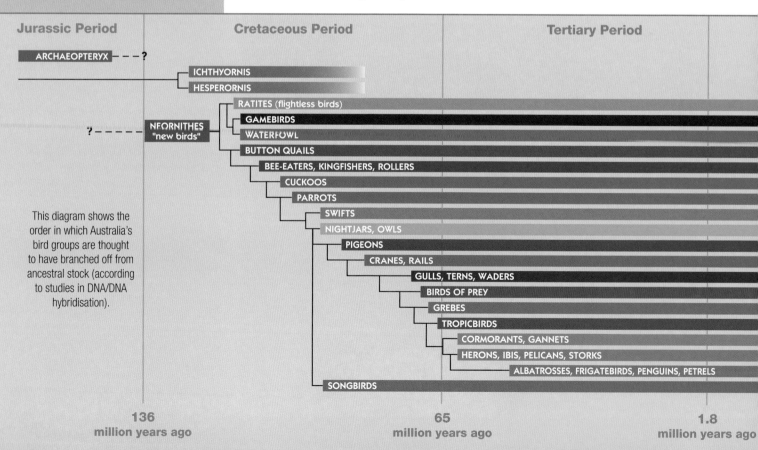

Jurassic Period	Cretaceous Period	Tertiary Period

ARCHAEOPTERYX – – – ?

ICHTHYORNIS
HESPERORNIS

RATITES (flightless birds)
GAMEBIRDS
? – – – – NEORNITHES "new birds"
WATERFOWL
BUTTON QUAILS
BEE-EATERS, KINGFISHERS, ROLLERS
CUCKOOS
PARROTS
SWIFTS
NIGHTJARS, OWLS
PIGEONS
CRANES, RAILS
GULLS, TERNS, WADERS
BIRDS OF PREY
GREBES
TROPICBIRDS
CORMORANTS, GANNETS
HERONS, IBIS, PELICANS, STORKS
ALBATROSSES, FRIGATEBIRDS, PENGUINS, PETRELS
SONGBIRDS

This diagram shows the order in which Australia's bird groups are thought to have branched off from ancestral stock (according to studies in DNA/DNA hybridisation).

136 million years ago

65 million years ago

1.8 million years ago

MOST PEOPLE know a bird by its common name (such as Laughing Kookaburra) but common names for the same species may change around the world. To make identification easier, each species also has a scientific name, which is usually derived from Greek or Latin and remains the same worldwide. The first name is the genus name and the second, the species name — *Dacelo novaeguineae* for the Laughing Kookaburra. This system of giving animals a two-word scientific name is known as binomial nomenclature.

BIRD BIOLOGY

All birds are vertebrates — like mammals and reptiles they have a backbone that acts as the framework for the central nervous system. Like humans, birds have a four-chambered heart, but their hearts beat much faster than ours do and their metabolic rate is much higher because flying expends enormous amounts of energy. Flying also consumes at least 25% more oxygen, so a bird's lungs have an extra set of veins running from the lungs to the heart and are much more efficient than a human's lungs. Birds' bodies also have air sacs that trap oxygen in the body to circulate it through the lungs and bloodstream for longer.

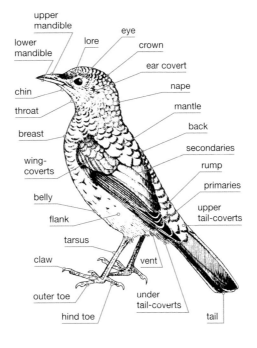

Birds are endothermic, which means they are warm-blooded and can regulate their body temperature. Humans usually have a body temperature of about 37°C, but a bird's body temperature is much higher at around 41°C. Birds also have minor adjustments to the circulatory system, known as miracle nets, which help them maintain body temperature. These miracle nets are areas in the head and legs where veins and arteries are intertwined; this allows warm blood in the arteries travelling to the bird's head or legs to warm up cooler blood in the veins returning to the heart.

Despite sharing some features with mammals, birds also have some characteristics that are more reptile-like. They lay eggs (rather than give birth to live young) and the feathers that cover their bodies are actually modified scales. However, along with wings and feathers, birds have many other features that set them apart from both mammals and reptiles. Birds have no bladder; instead, a vent leads to the cloaca, which functions as both their waste and reproductive organ. Their kidneys are larger (for their size) than a human's, and are connected to three pairs of renal arteries (where humans have a single pair).

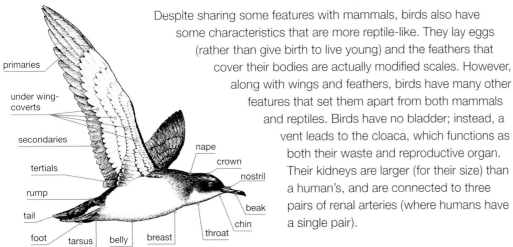

the FACTS!

BIRDS' HEARTS beat much faster than ours do. The average human heart beats at 72 beats per minute, the sparrow's heart at 460 and the tiny hummingbird's at an amazing 615 beats per minute!

PARROTS AND OSTRICHES lack a gall bladder, and cockatoos and parrots have no appendix.

BIRDS DON'T HAVE TEETH; instead, many keep stones or grit in the gizzard to grind up food and aid digestion. Fish-eating species, such as gulls and penguins, do not need a gizzard. Many species also have a "crop" — a muscular sac that stores food in the oesophagus so it can be regurgitated and fed to young later.

WHEN IT IS COLD, some species, such as mistletoebirds and nightjars, maintain their body heat by going into torpor.

OWLS' DENSE, warm feathers mean they can survive on 30% less food than other similar-sized bird species.

BIRDS EVOLVED BEAKS because they are lighter than toothed jaws and birds need to stay light to fly.

BIRDS DO NOT REALLY have true tails. Their tail feathers are simply attached to a bone, called the pygostyle, at the end of the spine.

FEMALE BIRDS possess WZ sex chromosomes, while males possess ZZ chromosomes. For humans and other mammals, the opposite applies. Females have XX sex chromosomes, while males have XY sex chromosomes.

Feathers
& features

Australian Ringneck

Crimson Rosella

Feathers are remarkable structures that allow birds an aerodynamic advantage over other species, as well as giving them their colourful plumage. However, birds are not only beautiful, they are also relatively intelligent animals.

THE INCREDIBLE FEATHER

Amazingly, feathers are just modified scales. Feathers make up at least 10% of a bird's body mass. They are made of keratin — like human fingernails and hair — and insulate birds as well as enabling them to fly. The largest and most abundant feathers are the "contour feathers", which comprise all of the flight feathers and many of the feathers on the body. The shape of a bird's contour feathers are important to its flight ability. Each contour feather has a hollow base (the calamus), which is embedded in the skin; the shaft (or rachis), which has projecting barbs; and smaller projections that come off the barbs, known as barbules. Combined, the barbs and barbules form the feathery vane of the feather.

Down feathers are the short, soft feathers that can be fluffed up to trap insulating air. Many chicks are covered with natal down, but even adult birds have down feathers underlying the contour feathers. Other feathers, known as semiplumes, are as long as contour feathers but have the soft, wispy barbs of down feathers. Even the thin, hair-like structures around some bird's faces are feathers — these are known as vibrissae. Vibrissae are extremely touch-sensitive; their primary function is to help enhance nocturnal birds' senses in the dark. Feathers do not regenerate. Over time, they wear out and become tatty and damaged. Lice can also destroy a bird's feathers and sometimes up to twelve species of feather-lice live on a single bird. To get around this, most birds moult at least once a year — losing all of their old feathers and regrowing new ones. Moulting requires a lot of protein in order to regrow feathers.

PERSONALISED FLIGHT PLANS

Flying is vitally important to all but Australia's largest bird species. It enables birds to seek food, shelter and mates; hence, many of a bird's body features are structurally modified to encourage flight. The forelimbs have become wings, with the "hand" and "finger" bones fusing to become the wing structure for primary flight feathers, and secondary flight feathers on the "forearm". To keep birds light enough to fly, the skull and bones contain air cavities, making them hollow. These are called "pneumatic bones" and are reinforced with struts inside the cavities to make them both light and strong. Other features are the "wishbone", and the keeled sternum where the strong wing muscles attach to the body.

Different flight requirements and styles lead to differences in wing structure. Birds that fly short distances in rapid bursts usually have short, rounded wings. Migratory birds ("frequent flyers") mostly have long, pointed wings. Some species have slotted wing tips for enhanced manoeuvrability. The largest flying bird species in the world is the Wandering Albatross, which weighs approximately 16 kg. Birds that weigh more than 18 kg, such as cassowaries and Emus, are too heavy to fly.

THE BRIGHT AND THE BEAUTIFUL

Feather colours have specific purposes, ranging from identification between species to camouflage. But where do the colours come from? In cross-section, feather barbs have three layers. The outer layer is transparent and can be clear or contain yellow, red or orange hues derived from organic carotenoids ingested from plants. Below this is another transparent layer that is either clear or contains tiny air bubbles that reflect blue light in an effect known as Tyndall scattering (the same phenomenon makes the sky appear blue). When the outer layer is yellow and the second layer reflects blue, the combination makes the feather appear green. The third layer contains granules of melanin, which can be black, brown or rufous. Scientists have recently discovered another fascinating quality — fluorescence. Researchers at the University of Queensland's Vision, Touch and Hearing Research Centre have found that some Budgerigar (above) feathers absorb ultraviolet light and glow in the dark, which helps budgies attract mates. Potential partners ignored budgies that had their feathers dulled by sunscreen, proving that budgies believe bright is beautiful.

NOT SUCH BIRDBRAINS!

Contrary to popular belief, birds are actually quite intelligent and have complex brains. Many species can use tools, some can imitate human speech and others can even count! The "birdbrained" concept came about because more than 100 years ago the bird's brain was thought to be made up largely of basal ganglia, which scientists believed was responsible for primitive and instinctive behaviour. We now know that birds' brains are more similar to human brains than first thought and

The Black-breasted Buzzard has been seen using tools to crack tough Emu eggs. This intelligent hawk picks up stones in its beak and hurls them at the eggs until the shells crack.

that the basal ganglia region of the brain does not just control primitive behaviour. Some birds, such as the corvids (crows, ravens and relatives), show a level of cognition more complex than that found in many mammal species.

A BIRD'S-EYE VIEW

Sight is a bird's keenest sense. Although the structure of a bird's eye is similar to that of humans, birds see a much broader spectrum of colour, including ultraviolet light. Birds' eyeballs are large compared to their bodies and their flatter retinas have more areas associated with sharp focus. The most important feature of bird eyesight is the presence of pecten — a vascular projection that supplies nutrients to the retina and is found only in birds. Its exact purpose is unknown, although it is thought that by having no blood vessels on the retina itself (which obstruct sight), birds are able to gain a much clearer perspective of the world.

the FACTS!

SCIENTISTS DISCOVERED that fluorescent head and cheek markings on budgerigars made their "chromatic signal" to a potential mate 14% more visible.

STUDIES INTO THE FEEDING habits of Scrub Jays in the UK proved that some birds are brainy enough to plan for the future. Researchers fed the jays from the same compartment each morning. They then mixed up the schedule by feeding the birds an evening meal in either their usual "breakfast" compartment or a different "dinner" compartment. They found the jays were less likely to store the evening meal when it was served in their "breakfast" compartment (knowing they would be guaranteed a meal in that compartment the following morning). When the experiment was changed and the birds were given two types of food, each from different compartments, they hid the foods in the other compartment — planning for the future likelihood of one type of food being unavailable.

BIRDS HAVE A THIRD EYELID, known as a "nictitating membrane" (below). This semi-transparent cover serves to protect the bird's eyes. Diving birds can close their nictitating membranes just before they hit the water.

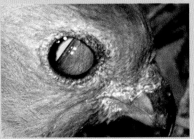

M & I MORCOMBE

SNIPE HAVE HIGH-SET EYES, giving them 360° vision.

BIRDS CANNOT SWIVEL their eyeballs, they have to turn their heads to see around them.

Avian
adaptations

Brown Honeyeater

the FACTS!

AUSTRALIA'S NECTAR-EATING SPECIES are often larger than those found in South American countries.

EXPLOITING DIETARY NICHES is one way some birds ensure they have plenty of food. Rainbow Bee-eaters (below) are able to feast on the stinging insects other birds ignore because they have learned how to hold the bee in their beaks and scrape it on a branch or rock to remove the sting.

THE ENDEMIC Magpie Goose has a beak that is sharply turned down at the tip — a modification that allows the birds to tug out the roots of certain water plants when foraging underwater.

LONG-BILLED BIRDS (such as snipe) have sensitive touch receptors attached to nerves in their beaks. When poking their beaks underwater, they can actually feel what lies below.

Birds' bodies have not just evolved as flying machines. Other parts of their anatomy have adapted to give birds the best chance of survival in a range of habitats and on a number of different diets. Over time, birds have also learned strategies and defence behaviours that give them a fighting chance at life.

THE BEST BEAK FOR THE JOB

A bird's beak is not just its mouth, it is a very effective tool that is able to dismember prey or probe sticky, nectar-producing flowers. Whether beak or bill, curved or straight, hooked or upturned, birds' modified mouths suit the food source they most frequently exploit.

Birds of prey, such as the Wedge-tailed Eagle, have sharply curved beaks designed for tearing chunks of flesh from prey. Long, curved beaks are usually found on bird species that are nectarivores, such as the Yellow-bellied Sunbird. They survive by sucking up the sticky sweetness from grass-trees, banksias, grevilleas, bottlebrushes, eucalypts and tea-trees. In return for their nectar, the plants are pollinated by the birds. Australia has many nectarivores but not one European plant species relies on birds for pollination.

Seed-eaters like mannikins and finches have short, strong cone-shaped beaks that are used to crush open the hard or fibrous coverings of grass seeds or the keratinous shells of insects. Dagger-like, pointed bills found on herons and egrets are employed as sharp spears for stabbing fish. Other underwater feeders, such as the Red-necked Avocet, dredge their submerged bills from side to side just above and parallel to the bottom of shallow watercourses to search for prey. The bill's upturned shape may help the avocet avoid the mud and silt and also allow it to snatch up prey near the surface.

Parrots have strong, sharply curved beaks and manoeuvrable tongues to help them crack open hard nuts and manipulate the kernel. A prominent feature of waterfowl is the flat, often broad, bill. A duck's bill is used to sift through water, silt and mud while searching for seeds, stems of water plants and small fishes and crustaceans. However, different dietary requirements have led to subsequent differences in beak shape. Grazers, such as the Australian Wood Duck and Cape Barren Goose, have shorter bills.

Clockwise from top right: Red-necked Avocet; Bush Stone-curlew; Royal Spoonbill; Gouldian Finch; Blue-winged Kookaburra; White-bellied Sea-Eagle; Southern Cassowary.

FEET TO FIT EACH LIFESTYLE

Foot and toe shape is also a good indicator of a particular bird species' lifestyle. Passerines are easily distinguished by their "perching feet" (right) that have three forwards-facing toes and one opposable backwards-facing toe to allow them to grip on to branches. Raptors have a similar four-toed foot (above left), although slightly varied because only two of their toes face forwards (one faces backwards and the other can face forwards or backwards).

Parrots, which are adept at grasping and prising open pine cones and palm nuts, have a strong grasping foot with two toes facing forwards and two backwards (left).

To propel themselves through the water, ducks have three forwards-facing webbed toes (above centre) and a small, high hind toe. Similar swimmers, such as pelicans, have all four webbed toes pointing forwards for maximum propulsion. Waterbirds also use their feet as brakes when they land.

Birds that "walk on water", such as swamphens and jacanas, have long, slender toes with three forwards-facing toes and one toe that points backwards (above right) to enable them to walk over thin lily pads and water plants.

BEHAVIOURAL STRATEGIES FOR SURVIVAL

Drought or seasonal flooding can have a big impact on bird numbers, as can fire and other natural disasters. Many bird species, however, find their greatest threat comes from predators. Successful bird species have developed ways to minimise risks and increase their chances of survival. Some birds, such as raptors, have even come to benefit from events that prove fatal for other species. Following bushfire, birds of prey swoop down to feast on the dead, dying and exposed. Likewise, while seasonal flooding might be devastating for some ground-dwelling species, it proves a boon for waterfowl and waders, which flock to temporary wetlands to feed and breed.

Top to bottom: A Brown Falcon searches for barbecued morsels after bushfire; Crested Terns seek safety in numbers.

Birds at greatest risk from predators may use camouflage and colouring, playing dead or injured or "ganging up" to avoid predation. Noisy Miners are particularly well-known for banding together to scare off other birds. Forming flocks or colonies has the advantage of many keen eyes on guard; when a threat approaches an alarm call can be sounded, allowing others to escape.

the FACTS!

CUCKOOS, PARROTS, cockatoos, owls and nightjars have two toes facing backwards and two facing forwards on each foot — a feature that is known as "zygodactylus"; others birds have just three toes and the ostrich has just two.

INCREDIBLY, TROPICBIRDS are unable to walk because their legs are too far back on their bodies. To move around on land they launch themselves forward with both feet and "plop" onto their bellies.

PELECANIFORMES share one thing in common — they all have "totipalmate" feet, which means that all four of their toes are connected by webbing.

WHEN WATERHOLES DRY UP, Black Swans may flock together and fly in V-formation to new watering holes. They are most often recorded flying by night, which makes sense given their black colouring.

THE LARGE, BRIGHT orange-yellow mouth and staring yellow eyes of the Tawny Frogmouth can sometimes scare off predators.

GROUND-NESTING BIRDS lead would-be predators away from the eggs with elaborate play-acting. A plover parent will pretend to have a broken wing to entice a fox away from its helpless chicks. Once the fox has been led away, the plover immediately recovers and flies back to its nest.

Bird
behaviour

Red-winged
Parrot

Feathers require regular preening, plumping and cleaning, but birds also engage in other avian behaviour that includes singing, dancing, roosting and, sometimes, long distance travelling.

A BIRD'S BEHAVIOUR depends largely on its lifestyle. Most birds are diurnal, which means they are awake during the day and sleep or roost at night. However, most owls are nocturnal and are very rarely seen by day. Some ground-dwelling birds, such as brush-turkeys and the Pheasant Coucal, retire to trees or shrubs to roost at night. Whereas some birds are solitary, or found in small family groups, others seek safety in numbers — forming large flocks or, in the case of seabirds, noisy, crowded colonies.

BATHING & PREENING

Birds keep their plumage bright and clean in a number of ways. Some bathe in rain showers, puddles, creeks or birdbaths. Others are lucky enough to have "self-conditioning" powder-down feathers. When preened, powder-down feathers produce a powder that helps maintain the feathers' condition. Other species produce preen oil, which is spread over the feathers and helps water to bead off, preventing the bird from becoming waterlogged. Recent studies suggest that preen oils may also affect a bird's smell, particularly during breeding season. Waterbirds, such as penguins, have very tightly packed feather barbs, making their feathers water-resistant rather than simply water-repellent.

the FACTS!

STUDIES HAVE SHOWN that it is possible for birds to be "half asleep". When they do this, half of the brain remains alert while the other half shows the slowed brain waves associated with sleep. The eye controlled by the "sleeping" half of the brain is closed, while the other eye stays open!

EPHRAHIM GARCIA, from Cornell University in New York, has been working on a design to create a "perching plane" based on the way birds settle on a branch. By mimicking the action birds make when they land — angling the wings against the airflow, while simultaneously flaring and lowering the tail to maximise drag — Garcia hopes to design a surveillance aircraft that can be brought to a perching standstill on a tall building.

WHY DON'T BIRDS fall off their perches when they sleep? Because, when their legs are bent, their toes lock into place and cannot be released until the legs are straightened again.

A Wonga Pigeon enjoys a bath, which helps keep feathers free from dust and parasites.

Barbs on the vanes of contour feathers need to be regularly "zipped" into place.

Crested Terns are long-distance flyers.

MIRACULOUS MIGRATION

There is much debate about how some birds manage to navigate their way hundreds of thousands of kilometres to breeding or feeding grounds. Scientists believe migratory birds can navigate using the sun or the position of the sunset and the stars at night. Alternatively, they may use the Earth's magnetic field as a map. Studies have even shown that homing pigeons simply follow their nose, creating a sensory "smell map" of the places they have been to.

The energetic courtship ritual of the male Superb Lyrebird involves dancing and singing melodies composed of mimicked sounds.

A male Victoria's Riflebird in display posture exposes his iridescent neck.

SONG & DANCE

Birds use singing and dancing displays to attract mates as well as to deter threats or competitors. Perhaps the most famous dancers of the Australian bush are lyrebirds and the Brolga. A lyrebird's magnificent fan-shaped tail is brought forwards over its head and shimmied, like a silvery filigree curtain, to impress females. Tall, graceful Brolgas perform an elaborate mating dance that includes bowing, prancing and dramatically flinging grass or twigs into the air.

Songbirds, which are also known as passerines, are renowned for their beautiful carolling. A bird's voicebox is not its larynx; instead, birds have an extra feature called a syrinx, which sits at the junction of the bird's windpipe and bronchii and creates sounds as air resonates across a thin membrane. This gives birds two chambers for making sounds, allowing them to sing two distinct notes simultaneously.

THE ORIGIN OF SONG

Approximately 5700 species of bird are passerines and it was at first thought that these songbirds originated in Europe, or at least that Australasian and Eurasian species evolved independently. Using DNA research collected from 144 singing species, scientists from the University of Minnesota in America have now discovered that songbirds originated in the giant supercontinent Gondwana, which later split to become Australia, Antarctica and New Zealand. From around 65 million years ago, some of these songbirds began to spread to Asia from Australia, while others, such as flycatchers, spread from New Zealand to South America.

the FACTS!

BELLBIRDS' "SILVER-VOICED" tinkling call sounds beautiful to us, but all other birds hear is the warning "keep away"!

IT IS A WELL-KNOWN FACT that male songbirds sing to attract a mate, but what about females? A recent study of European bird species conducted at the University of Antwerp, Belgium, showed that the females of many species (101 of the 109 researched) also sang. The researchers later found, after tracing these species' evolutionary history, that females evolved the ability to sing first! They may have used their songs to stop other females entering their territory or to attract males.

PLAIN-TAILED WRENS in Ecuador sing the most complex songs known in the animal world. Up to seven singers join in complex choruses and males and females add their voices on cue.

BIRDS OF THE SAME SPECIES are not all singing the same songs! Evidence of regional "dialects" and "accents" have been found in Australian Eastern Whipbirds and in Golden Bowerbirds. Birdsong is regarded as a "cultural" attribute — it is learned rather than innate. For this reason, birds from isolated areas may have regional variations in their songs. Strangely, in the case of the whipbirds, the females' songs differed while the males' songs remained the same. This may be because the male whipbird's "whipcrack" is hard to perform and therefore easily impresses females.

TWEET DREAMS!

A study conducted at the University of Chicago found that Australian Zebra Finches "rehearse" their songs while they sleep. To discover this, they measured the patterns of brain neuron activity associated with singing during the day and then measured the same areas of the brain at night. They found that activity in this region while the finches were asleep was a type of "song replay" facility to help the bird learn new songs or rehearse songs.

PETER SLATER

13

Getting
together

Like all animals, birds are driven by a desire to reproduce. Mating calls, sometimes-bizarre courtship rituals and biological cues (in the form of eye-catching mating plumage) help birds find a partner. A few species even try to entice a mate by building a bower or offering food.

MIGRATORY SPECIES sometimes travel thousands of kilometres to meet up with the same partner and return to the same nesting site each year. Individuals of more stationary species usually establish a territory and then use singing and display behaviour to attract potential mates and deter competition.

STICKING TOGETHER

Most bird species — up to 90% in fact — are surprisingly monogamous, with a male and female pairing up for at least one breeding season and many species choosing the same partner for life. Only when their partner dies, or after numerous breeding failures, will they move on to another partner.

Many of the Pelecaniformes, especially, return to the same nest site year after year and mate with the same partner. Wandering Albatrosses might literally wander, but their eyes do not — despite travelling long distances, these birds remain faithful to the same partner for life.

Clockwise from top left: Rainbow Bee-eaters; Purple-crowned Fairy-wrens; Little Penguins; Rainbow Lorikeets; Royal Albatrosses; Eclectus Parrots.

the FACTS!

MALE MAGPIE GEESE can have up to three female partners, which all lay their eggs in the same nest and then incubate the eggs in turn.

A MALE TERN will often show a prospective female a fresh fish, but will not give it to her on the first "date" — only when they have formed a pair bond will he feed her.

IN MOST PARROT SPECIES, males have more vivid plumage than females. Only a few species, such as the Eclectus Parrot (below), have a female that is more brightly coloured. Usually, when females are more brightly coloured it is due to an avian role reversal where the female must compete for mates. However, uniquely, this is not the case with the Eclectus Parrot. Researchers have discovered that colour is influenced by lifestyle in these parrots. Because nesting hollows are so scarce, the female's crimson colouring can help make her conspicuous in the tree tops to fend off competition. Males, with their green plumage, are better camouflaged, which may help them hide from predators.

M & I MORCOMBE

RON & VALERIE TAYLOR

PLAYING THE FIELD

Birds that leave their partners to incubate eggs and raise chicks alone while they go in search of other mates are known as "polygamous" species. Polygamous birds are usually those in which the male is significantly more brightly plumed than the female. However, in some "polyandrous" species the females are the ones that seek more than one partner. Female Emus, Southern Cassowaries and Comb-crested Jacanas have many partners and leave the males to sit on their eggs. DNA research is also proving that some species are less faithful than they were once thought to be. Swans were believed to be the very model of avian loyalty, but recent DNA studies on female Black Swans found that one in six Black Swan cygnets was not the biological offspring of its supposed "father". Researchers at the University of Melbourne are fitting Black Swans in Melbourne's Albert Park Lake with tracking devices to see just how female swans go about this extracurricular mating and what factors might affect the mates they choose.

To impress females, Satin Bowerbirds decorate a bower made of sticks with blue objects.

THE BIRDS & THE BEES

Once a bird has found a suitable partner, all that remains is to consummate the relationship by mating. From a reproductive perspective, birds have more in common with reptiles than with mammals. Male birds do have testes that produce sperm, but these are concealed inside the body. Males of most species have just three small nodules on the front lip of the cloaca, rather than any sort of penis. The nodules swell with lymphatic fluid and control the direction of sperm when it is spurted out of the cloaca. Only some waterfowls and ratite species have a cloaca that is modified to form a rudimentary penis. Female birds have two ovaries, but in almost all bird species only the ovary on the left is functional. When birds reproduce, males evert their cloacas so the sperm can be transferred to the female. Eggs are fertilised in the female's upper oviduct, and as each egg passes along the oviduct layers of albumen (or egg white) are deposited on it. In the uterus, the shell and pigment are added.

Male Superb Fairy-wrens "furgle", or sneak into a neighbour's territory bearing gifts for females.

the FACTS!

ENVIRONMENTAL CONDITIONS determine when, and sometimes where, certain species breed. In seasonally dry areas, waterfowl may breed at times to coincide with floods or monsoonal weather.

THE GREAT FRIGATEBIRD'S colourful throat pouch (below) is inflated to attract females. Males also clap their beaks and wave their wings around. Sometimes these birds gather in groups of around 30 males and try to "outdo" each other when females pass overhead.

MARTIN HARVEY/ANT PHOTO

MOST WATERFOWLS MATE IN THE WATER, but Cape Barren Geese mate on dry land. They perform a strange, head-bowing mating dance that is known as "waltzing". Cape Barren Geese are sometimes also called Pig Geese because males make a loud grunting sound when courting.

YOUNG SATIN BOWERBIRD females may be impressed by the male's blue-adorned bower, but research has shown that older females look for a male who can also strut his stuff. Scientists affixed blue tiles and objects to bowers, which appealed to females under three years of age. Older females were more likely to care less about the interior design and more about the male's display of running back and forth across the bower while emitting loud buzzing calls.

Eggs, nests
& chicks

Eggs were an extremely important development in allowing animals to move away from the water to reproduce. However, simple structures still had to be created to stop the eggs from rolling or breaking and to provide a temporary home for chicks. As a result, birds developed many clever ways of making nests.

the FACTS!

EMU EGGS (right) are the largest native bird eggs found in Australia and may weigh as much as 700 g.

THE COLOUR OF EGGS varies depending on the species of bird and where they are laid. Those that are well hidden in deep nests or in tree hollows are often white, while speckled eggs are better camouflaged for species that lay eggs on pebbles or sand. Birds that lay eggs on reeds or plant matter usually have eggs that have a confusing "scribbled" pattern.

FAIRY MARTINS use their bills to collect mud and patch together a bottle-shaped nest of mud and saliva (left). Fairy Martins build these nests in large colonies, with many hundreds of mud-brick nests clustered along a cliff, under bridges or under the eaves of some buildings.

NESTING BIRDS are usually particular about where they build. Some, however, are adaptable. The Black Noddy (below) has chosen this elevated window sill as the site for its nest.

ALL BIRDS LAY eggs, which come in an assortment of sizes and colours. Eggs are fascinating, strong structures that are composed from a single cell — the biggest cell in the animal kingdom! These capsule-like structures are designed to protect the growing embryo when it is at its most vulnerable. Eggshells are semi-permeable, meaning that air and moisture are able to pass through them. They are also water-resistant. Inside the shell, the chorion encloses the chick and all of the other structures that support it, including the egg yolk, which is actually the food sac for the growing embryo. The albumen (or egg white) cushions the embryo and provides it with water. The embryo itself floats in a membranous sac of amniotic fluid, which alleviates the need for a watery environment for young to be produced.

Diagram labels: waste sac · yolk · yolk sac · membrane · air space · eggshell · egg membrane · shell membrane · embryo · albumen (egg white)

THE YOUNG & THE HELPLESS

A baby bird breaks its way out of the encasing eggshell using a hard projection on the beak known as an "egg tooth". The egg tooth falls off soon after the chick hatches. Chicks that are born with feathers and are independent when they hatch are known as "precocial". Precocial chicks come from eggs that have a high yolk content compared with the eggs of other species. When they hatch, precocial chicks have 15–30% of the egg's yolk in their gut — this nourishes them until they find food. Most megapodes, such as the Australian Brush-turkey and Malleefowl, have precocial chicks. Chicks that hatch blind and featherless (above) need parental care until they are fully feathered and can begin to fly and feed themselves — these are referred to as "altricial" young. On the other hand, "nidicolous" chicks remain in the nest for only a little while after they hatch. Chicks that spend a long time in the nest often have to amuse themselves while their parents go in search of food. Booby chicks spend a lot of time catching pebbles, shells and other beach debris that they toss in the air. This kind of "practice play" enables them to learn the vital skills they will need as adults to make nests and catch fish.

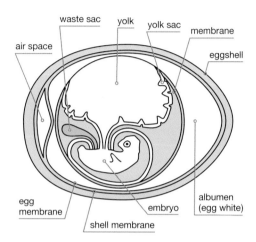

M & I MORCOMBE

A woven, grassy nest among reeds allows Long-tailed Finches to keep their chicks warm, secure and well hidden.

Comb-crested Jacana eggs are incubated by the male on a flimsy, floating nest made of reeds and water lilies scraped together.

BIRD NURSERIES

To further protect their eggs and help keep them warm, birds instinctively build nests. When it comes to avian architecture, like most other aspects of their lives, birds are remarkably resourceful. Bird nurseries come in all shapes, sizes and locations and a range of materials are used to help make the nest cosy and strong. Birds that construct nests of twigs or gathered material may make hundreds of collecting missions to furnish the nest. Seabirds and waterbirds, which sometimes have limited access to trees and sticks, often simply lay their eggs in a scratched-out shallow hollow in the ground. Usually, one of these bird parents must sit on the egg at all times to stop the exposed egg becoming an easy target for predators. Mud, tree hollows, reeds and grasses, pebbles, moss, feathers — and even saliva and bird poo — are used as construction materials.

DOMESTIC DUTIES

With the exception of some polygamous and polyandrous birds, as well as female megapodes, the work is far from over once the egg has been laid into the nest. Because birds are warm-blooded, the developing chick inside the egg usually has to be kept warm by incubation. Sometimes, both parents take responsibility for the task; other times only one parent will remain with the eggs and feed the hungry chicks once they emerge. Cooperative breeding makes the task of chick rearing easier for some species, with additional helpers sharing feeding duties.

In most cases, chicks are fed either partly digested food by regurgitation or solid food that is given to them directly. Baby birds frequently squabble over food and the smallest, weakest chick sometimes dies of starvation or bullying while still in the nest. Ducklings and cygnets, however, are able to feed themselves shortly after hatching.

Masked Boobies commonly lay two eggs about six days apart on flat, exposed areas of islands.

Some of the most impressive nests are the raptors' huge eyries perched high in the trees.

the FACTS!

TO MAKE A CUP-SHAPED NEST, birds first pile their raw materials on top, placing soft feathers or grasses on the inside. They then sit in the nest and continue to turn around and around until they form a nice, firm cup.

A UNIQUE FEATURE of pigeons and doves is that they produce "crop milk" to feed their young. This is not really milk but a kind of thick, soupy protein and fat. The mother pigeon eventually weans her chicks onto seeds by storing seeds in the crop where they soak in the milk to form an easy-to-eat porridge.

AFTER BREEDING in Australia's southern regions, Short-tailed Shearwater parents abandon their fat, fluffy chicks and set off alone on a 15,000 km voyage to Antarctica.

MANY BIRD SPECIES, such as the Eastern Yellow Robin (below), feed their chicks largely on insects because chicks need lots of protein to grow feathers.

Flightless wonders
— Emus & cassowaries

Order: Struthioniiformes
Family: Casuariidae

Large, flightless ratites, such as Southern Cassowaries and Emus, probably evolved from flying birds that lived in environments with few predators. Over time, they lost the need for flight and grew bigger.

EMUS AND CASSOWARIES are related, but perhaps only distantly. Some scientists estimate that the Emu diverged from the same ancestral line as the cassowary around 35 million years ago. At this time, a bird named *Emuarius* existed and showed some features of both Emus and cassowaries. Unlike birds that can fly, ratites have a flat (rather than keeled) breastbone because they do not need their wing muscles (pectorals) to attach to the breastbone.

Emus inhabit savanna woodland and sclerophyll forest across much of the Australian mainland. Their numbers have probably increased since European settlement because dams and bores have given them more access to water.

Tracking data suggests that a single Emu can travel more than 900 km in a nine-month period. Fathers with chicks in tow travel much slower.

the FACTS!

THE EMU is the second-tallest bird in the world. Fully grown Emus may weigh as much as 30–45 kg and stand 1.6–2 m tall.

SCIENTISTS ESTIMATE that ratites lost the power of flight only around 10 million years ago. Of all of the living ratite species in the world, the Australian Emu has the least developed wings.

AUSTRALIA WAS ONCE HOME to two dwarf Emu species that inhabited Kangaroo Island, South Australia, and King Island, Tasmania. Unfortunately, they are now extinct.

THE EMU'S SCIENTIFIC NAME, *Dromaius novaehollandiae,* translates as "swift-footed bird of New Holland". Emus can run very fast when they need to, reaching speeds of up to 50 km/h; but as they are nomadic, Emus prefer to walk slowly from one destination to the next to conserve energy.

SURPRISINGLY, EMU is not an Aboriginal word. The word is probably taken from the Arabic for "large bird" and was first used by Portuguese explorers to describe cassowaries.

EMUS ARE STRONG SWIMMERS and can even cross wide rivers.

MR MUM

Female Emus are more dominant than males. They are also noisier. When ready to breed, females inflate their air sacs and resonate them to make a loud booming signal to attract males. Although the female Emu lays the eggs, which each usually weigh around 700 g, it is the male Emu that plays mum.

Male Emus sit on a clutch of eggs for 8 weeks, standing up only to turn the eggs over occasionally. During this time they don't eat, drink or defecate. While incubating eggs, some males may lose as much as a third of their body weight!

During spring and summer, Emus "binge eat" to build up fat reserves because both males and females quit eating as soon as the breeding season starts. Once they hatch, chicks stay with their father until they are independent at 6–18 months of age.

Male Emus do not so much sit on the eggs as squat on them, with the toes poking out in front of the body. They remain there, through sunshine or rain, for eight weeks.

RARE RAINFOREST DWELLERS

Although there are three cassowary species worldwide (all of them existing in New Guinea), Australia is home to just one species, the Southern Cassowary (*Casuarius casuarius*). These large, distinctive birds are fruit-lovers that inhabit the tropical rainforests and rainforest edges of north Queensland.

Like Emus, they are unable to fly; however, to negotiate their dense rainforest environment they have an added tool — a hard helmet known as a casque, which they use to "head-butt" their way through tangled vines and undergrowth.

To help males and females recognise each other amid the forest greenery, cassowaries also have bright blue necks and large red flaps of skin under the neck known as "wattles".

Top to bottom: Blue skin on the Southern Cassowary's neck helps it stand out in the green rainforest; Rainforest fruit, such as that of the Blue Quandong, is their favourite food.

FEEDING AGGRESSION

If threatened, cassowaries vigorously protect themselves and their young. However, feeding these large birds can also lead to a change in their behaviour, making them unusually competitive and cranky. The sharp, 12 cm, dagger-like claw on the back of the feet can do serious damage to a human. In 1926, one person who threatened a cassowary was even killed. Cassowaries can grow up to 1.75 m tall and weigh 70 kg, making them a formidable opponent. Queensland Parks and Wildlife Service believes that much of the threat comes from people feeding these giant, flightless wonders. Based on newspaper reports and eye-witness accounts, in the past twenty years QPWS estimates that 150 people have been attacked by cassowaries but that 75% of the attacks occurred when people were feeding or teasing the birds. Cassowaries should never be hand-fed as it makes them competitive and aggressive.

the FACTS!

THE WORD CASSOWARY comes from the Papuan words *kasu* (horned) and *weri* (head).

THE SOUTHERN CASSOWARY'S casque (above) may look bony, but it is more horn-like than bone-like and the inside is spongy, allowing it to act like a shock-absorber.

AFTER LAYING HER CLUTCH of three or four eggs, the female Southern Cassowary abandons them, leaving the male to incubate and care for chicks. This way, the female cassowary can mate with a number of males and lay up to three clutches of eggs during the breeding season. After 47–54 days, the eggs hatch and the chicks remain with their father for around nine months before they become independent.

A CASSOWARY CHICK (below) looks nothing like its doting dad. They are striped brown and white until they reach about three months old, and only grow the casque and brightly coloured wattle when they are older.

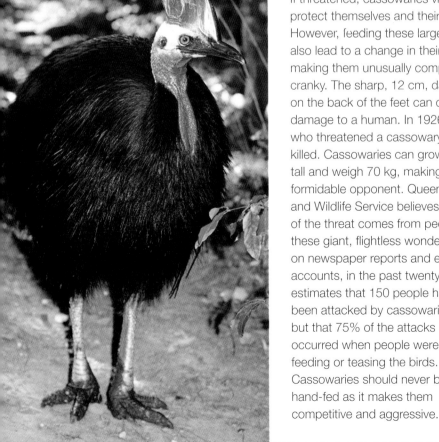

MARTIN WILLIS

Conservation Watch

All of Australia's grebe species are currently secure, although care must be taken to protect their freshwater habitats.

Grebes
— foot-propelled divers

Order: Podicipediformes
Family: Podicipedidae

Swimming and diving are both activities for which grebes are supremely well adapted. Their lobed, rather than webbed, feet are placed well back on their bodies, which makes walking tricky but swimming very easy.

the FACTS!

HESPERORNIS may have been the ancestor of modern grebes.

GREBES HAVE A PECULIAR habit of eating their own feathers. This may be a way of lining the stomach to prevent being poked by fish bones and may help form pellets of indigestible fish bones and scales. However, some scientists have suggested that it might also reduce gastric parasites such as worms.

A GREBE'S EGGS are pale blue and are laid in a floating nest of scraped together aquatic vegetation.

ORNITHOLOGISTS have long wondered at the bizarre courtship display of the Great Crested Grebe, which performs a fascinating "dance" that consists of both partners shaking their heads, crests erect, before the male dives to the bottom. He returns with a piece of weed in his mouth. Then both male and female turn, swim away and dive, each returning with a piece of weed. At this point, both birds perform the "penguin dance" — raising themselves up and, with their breasts touching, furiously paddling the water with their feet.

AUSTRALIA HAS THREE SPECIES of grebe. The smallest is the Australasian Grebe (*Tachybaptus novaehollandiae*) and the largest, the Great Crested Grebe (*Podiceps cristatus*). The other species is the Hoary-headed Grebe (*Poliocephalus poliocephalus*).

The fossil record indicates that true grebes first appeared about 23–25 million years ago (in the late Oligocene or early Miocene Epoch), although the lineage of these birds is still a matter of conjecture. Grebes are most at home on the water and build floating nests to breed. When on land, they stand upright and waddle. To escape danger, they quickly dive under the water. Most grebe species are also weak flyers, having only narrow wings, but some can fly long distances at night. Two species of South American grebe do not fly at all.

Left: A Great Crested Grebe sits on its loosely constructed nest of waterweed.

BUOYANCY ADJUSTERS

Grebes have very soft but dense overlapping feathers that stick out from their skin at right angles and curve around to overlap each other at the tip. Sleeking down or fluffing up these waterproof feathers allows the grebe to adjust its buoyancy in the water. Before a grebe dives, it presses its feathers to its body, which forces out air bubbles and provides a sleek, streamlined effect that can also allow the bird to swim below the water's surface with just its head and neck protruding.

Left and above: Australasian Grebes. When swimming, the lobed feet set well back on the body act as paddles to propel the grebe forward.

Wild waterfowl
— swans, ducks & geese

Order: Anseriformes
Families: Anseranatidae & Anatidae

There are approximately 150 species of waterfowl in the world and Australia's inland seas and brackish waterways are home to just nineteen of them. Some, such as the Cape Barren Goose, Pink-eared Duck and Freckled Duck, are endemic.

HARD, BROAD BILLS and webbed feet are the distinguishing features of waterfowl. Ducks and geese use their flat, modified beaks to filter small aquatic animals, seeds and plant roots from the water. On the inside edge of the bill are rows of hard, filtering plates called lamellae, which retain food as water passes through the beak. Grazing species, such as the Australian Wood Duck (*Chenonetta jubata*) and the Cape Barren Goose (*Cereopsis novaehollandiae*), have shorter, shearing beaks for pecking at grasses. Australia's unpredictable rainfall means that some waterfowl species may travel long distances between feeding and breeding areas. Other species may spend all their lives in one wetland area unless forced out by drought.

PLUMAGE FOR PAIRING UP

Unlike most avian species, which moult once a year, many waterfowl species moult twice — once to create colourful breeding plumage and then again once breeding season has ended. Most species pair bond for several years and many keep the same partner for life. Vivid breeding plumage may help to attract a partner, but it might also alert a predator, so their "everyday" plumage is usually much plainer. During post-nuptial moult, waterfowl are unable to fly — with the exception of the Magpie Goose (*Anseranas semipalmata*) — so moulting usually coincides with the time when they have offspring that are also unable to fly.

Top to bottom: Plumed Whistling-ducks (*Dendrocygna eytoni*); Cape Barren Goose; The Freckled Duck (*Stictonetta naevosa*) is Australia's rarest waterfowl species; Chestnut Teal (*Anas castanea*) fly in flocks.

the FACTS!

THE UNIQUE MAGPIE GOOSE has no close avian relatives. It has some duck-like and some goose-like features and its scientific name *Anseranas semipalmata* translates as "half-webbed goose-duck".

THE CROP of the Magpie Goose was a particular delicacy for Arnhem Land Aborigines who would "milk" grains of wild rice out of the crop of the bird and cook it to be served with the fire-roasted goose.

MUSK DUCKS (*Biziura lobata*) produce a strong, musky smelling preening oil, which has given them their name.

GEESE AND DUCKS were some of the first animals to be domesticated. Records show that Greylag Geese were domesticated as much as 450 years ago.

DESPITE THEIR NAME, pygmy-geese are actually ducks.

SOME WATERFOWL SPECIES that inhabit estuaries or saltwater wetlands are able to excrete excess salt through their nostrils.

ELEGANT AND UNUSUAL, Australia's Black Swan (*Cygnus atratus,* below) is the world's only swan species that is black. It is also Australia's largest waterfowl with a wingspan of up to 2 m. Black Swans are not entirely black — their flight feathers are long and white and their beaks are bright red.

Raptors
— birds of prey

Order: Falconiformes
Family: Accipitridae

Top left and above: The endemic Wedge-tailed Eagle (*Aquila audax*) is Australia's largest bird of prey. It can have a wingspan up to 2.5 m wide and can soar as high as 2000 m above the ground.

the FACTS!

SPLAYED or "fingered" feathers on the wing tips flex upwards to help raptors soar (above).

IN LATIN, the word "raptor" means "one who seizes and carries away".

A RAPTOR'S EYESIGHT is so efficient that it can spot a rabbit's ears twitching up to 3.2 km away! Raptors eyes can focus on three zones at once — the horizon on each side and a spot straight ahead.

AUSTRALIA'S SMALLEST eagle is the Little Eagle (*Hieraaetus morphnoides*, below), which has a wingspan of only about 120 cm.

GOSHAWKS and sparrowhawks are small raptors with broad wings that are rounded at the tips. They perch in the safety of woodland and rely on surprise to snatch up small mammals and other birds.

LETTER-WINGED KITES breed in large colonies during mouse and rat plagues.

Twenty-four fearsome native raptor species inhabit Australian skies and five are endemic to this continent. Australia's raptors belong to two families. The family Accipitridae comprises eagles and hawks. Falcons are placed in the family Falconidae.

WING SHAPE is dependent on a bird's habitat and lifestyle. Hawks that live in woodland have shorter wings that are more suited to manoeuvring between tree trunks as they fly. Soaring, open-air species (like eagles and kites) have long, broad wings with fingered tips. Each raptor group has a distinct wing shape that can help with identification. In silhouette, eagles have pointed heads and a large wingspan with fanned or spaced feathers on the wingtips. Kites have a similar wing shape, but a triangular tail. Harriers and goshawks have straight, longer tails and falcons have backward-facing wing tips. Tails are used for steering and braking but, because they produce drag, they can slow a raptor down.

EAGLE EYES, BEAKS & TALONS

Raptors have telephoto vision and excellent eyesight that is especially suited for detecting movement. Two special sections called foveas control a raptor's vision. The first fovea allows each eye to be directed sideways to scan (peripheral vision); the second enables both eyes to focus to the front to detect movement. Once prey is sighted, raptors immediately adjust their eyes' focus to home in on their meal. Raptors attack prey with powerful talons attached to tendons that keep their claws locked to prevent escape. After seizing and carrying off its prey, the raptor holds the meal in its talons and tears off strips with its curved beak. Bones, teeth, feathers and other indigestible body parts are regurgitated later in pellet form.

HIGH IN AN EYRIE

Eagles, Ospreys and the large kites build huge, conspicuous nests high in the tree tops, where their young will be protected from almost all predators. The nests (known as eyries) are made of sticks, twigs, bark and leaves and are renovated each year to add to their bulk.

Many raptor species mate for life. Before mating, males perform elaborate aerial displays to show off their hunting prowess and acrobatic ability. After mating, the female lays a clutch of eggs that she must incubate for approximately one month. Larger raptors may lay only one or two eggs, but some of the smaller species lay as many as five or six. During the incubation period, the female's partner brings her food. Even after the chicks hatch, she will remain on the nest until the chicks are old enough to be left while she hunts. Eagle chicks may remain in the nest for as long as three months. Some smaller raptor species begin to fly after a month.

FLYING KITES

Australia is home to six small raptors commonly known as kites and three of them — the Black-shouldered (*Elanus axillaris*), Letter-winged (*E. scriptus*) and Square-tailed Kite (*Lophoictinia isura*) — are found only in Australia. All are daytime hunters except for the Letter-winged Kite, which hunts at night. Kite species are particularly fond of dining on mice. When mice are in plague proportions, kites are able to breed more prolifically.

Left: A Square-tailed Kite and chick. Despite its name, this species is actually a hawk.

M & I MORCOMBE

MASTER FISHERS

The second-largest bird of prey in Australia is the White-bellied Sea-Eagle (*Haliaeetus leucogaster*). It inhabits coastal areas, where it swoops down from a perch in a high tree to feast on fish, sea snakes, turtles and other marine animals. Sharp bumps, called spicules, under their feet help them grasp slippery fish. They also occasionally prey on other birds and small mammals and can attack prey as large as a swan! Stealing a meal from another fish-eating bird is also a common tactic for the White-bellied Sea-Eagle.

the FACTS!

AN OSPREY (*Pandion haliaetus*, left) can seize and carry off prey that weighs more than itself.

THE OSPREY is the only raptor in the subfamily Pandioninae. It is a fish-eater and the only raptor with a reversible outer toe.

LARGE RAPTORS that require the power of flight all year round moult their feathers gradually so that they can always fly.

THE SPOTTED HARRIER (*Circus assimilis*, below) is the only harrier to nest in trees — all other harriers are ground-nesters. It creates a nest well hidden by foliage (often mistletoe) and surrounded by shrubbery.

THICK, SCALY SKIN on the White-bellied Sea-Eagle's legs help it avoid bites from venomous sea snakes, which it sometimes seizes and eats.

WHITE-BELLIED SEA-EAGLES make a loud honking call that sounds more like the noise of a goose than an eagle.

Falcons
— demons of speed

the FACTS!

Order: Falconiformes
Family: Falconidae

Falcons are small, sleek raptors distinguished by having wings that sweep back at the tip. They are the fastest of all raptors and Australia has six native species, of which two are endemic.

THE HARD, RAZOR-SHARP talons of raptors pierce through the prey's flesh and puncture its vital organs. Falcons sometimes also render their prey immobile by biting through its vertebrae.

RAPTORS, such as the Australian Hobby (below), are also food hoarders. They store any extra food and return to devour it later.

BIRDS made for speed (like falcons) have shorter tails, while those that need greater steering ability have longer tails.

THE BROWN FALCON (below) often uses the abandoned nests of crows or other birds of prey rather than building its own nest.

THE SMALLEST FALCON in Australia is the Nankeen Kestrel (*Falco cenchroides*) and the largest is the Black Falcon (*F. subniger*), which is actually a sooty brown and is frequently confused with the Brown Falcon (*F. berigora*). The Grey Falcon (*F. hypoleucos*) and the Black Falcon are both found only in Australia.

Distinguishing features of falcons are their backswept wings, bare rings of skin around the eyes and toothed bills. On each side of the beak, falcons have a "tooth" (or notched projection) that is purpose-built for slicing through their prey's neck.

SPIRAL OF DEATH

Often, one of the first signs that there is a falcon in the vicinity is the alarmed squawking from other birds that have spotted this sharp-eyed predator circling above. Falcons spend a lot of time circling high in the sky, scoping for prey. Once they have spotted a potential victim, they spiral in towards their quarry before swooping down. Scientists were unsure why falcons followed such a spiral path once they had prey in their sights, but suspected that the explanation had something to do with the bird's eyesight.

Laboratory tests suggested that falcons are able to see objects in front of them the most clearly when their heads were held at a 40° angle to one side. However, when flying, turning the head in this way would create friction that would slow the birds down. Spiralling in, although following a longer path, allows them to keep their eye on the target without slowing their speed.

Left: Nankeen Kestrels are common across mainland Australia.

Peregrine Falcon (*Falco peregrinus*) in flight

Peregrine Falcons are the world's fastest birds.

Conservation Watch

The Grey Falcon is vulnerable and is considered globally threatened. It has an estimated population of about 1000 breeding pairs.

GREAT AUSTRALIAN HOBBY

The Australian Hobby (*Falco longipennis*) is a small falcon with long, slender wings. The species name *longipennis* means "long feather". Unlike larger falcons, which feed on other birds and mammals, Australian Hobbies feed largely on small birds and insects. Nankeen Kestrels are also smaller than other falcons and prefer to feed on rodents and small mammals.

FLEDGLING FALCONS

Most falcons breed at around two years (for females) and three years (for males); however, young Nankeen Kestrels are sexually mature by one year of age. Falcons do not build their own nests, but use an old stick nest or steal a nest from its original owner by force. Fledgling falcons have longer flight feathers to help them learn to fly in their first year. Once they are able to fly and their ability to steer improves, their first-moult flight feathers become more tapered and less broad.

The regal Brown Falcon

CLIFFS & HIGHRISES

Peregrine Falcons (*Falco peregrinus*) will nest just about anywhere, including in an old stick nest built by crows or another raptor, on the window ledge of a tall building, on dam walls, in mine shafts or in small caves on cliff faces or overhangs up to 150 m above the ground. Once they have found a suitable nesting site, females usually lay three to five eggs and incubate them for around 33 days.

When the chicks hatch, they remain in the nest for 38–42 days. Even once they leave the nest they may remain in the nest area for up to eight months.

Left, top to bottom: Peregrine Falcons are opportunistic nesters; A Nankeen Kestral nesting in a cliff face.

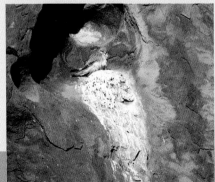

the FACTS!

THE WORD FALCON is derived from the same Latin stem as *falx*, which means "scythe" and refers to the bent-back shape of the bird's wings.

THE AUSTRALIAN HOBBY is fast enough to catch bats and flying-foxes in mid-flight.

THE PEREGRINE FALCON is the fastest bird in the world and can reach speeds of more than 200 km/h! It used to be the pride of falconers in the nineteenth and twentieth centuries before the practice was banned in Australia.

NANKEEN KESTRELS form breeding pairs that soar together in aerial displays, making mock parry and defence actions.

THE PEREGRINE FALCON feeds largely on birds that fly in flocks, such as pigeons, parrots and starlings. It sometimes hunts cooperatively in pairs. Peregrine Falcons (below) are often seen harassing larger birds.

25

Penguins
& tube-nosed birds

Orders: Sphenisciformes & Procellariiformes
Families: Spheniscidae, Diomedeidae & Procellariidae

The seas and oceans that lap Australia's 36,000 km coastline provide shelter and sustenance for many seabird species — both in the air and in the water.

the FACTS!

ALBATROSSES PAIR for life and use the same nest site each year. One egg is laid each season and both male and female albatrosses incubate the egg for approximately 79 days. Once hatched, albatross chicks reach maturity slowly and may not breed until they are five years old.

ALBATROSSES ARE MOSTLY found towards the Antarctic end of the Southern Hemisphere, where winds blow strongly all year round. Weak winds around the equator are known as the doldrums. Albatrosses find it difficult to glide when they are "in the doldrums".

AUSTRALIA'S RAREST NATIVE seabird is Gould's Petrel (*Pterodroma leucoptera*), which breeds on Cabbage Tree Island, New South Wales. A relocation program has resulted in some birds breeding on nearby Boondelbah Island.

THE MUTTONBIRD, or Short-tailed Shearwater, is the only Australian bird that can legally be harvested for food (below). Each year up to 400,000 of these fat, fluffy chicks are removed from their burrows and made into salted or canned meat. The soft down is then used as stuffing for eiderdowns, quilts and sleeping bags.

SOARING OVER THE OCEANS are the long-distance flyers of the order Procellariiformes, such as albatrosses, petrels, prions and shearwaters. Shearwaters are the most diverse family group and are typically about the size of small gulls. Petrels can be larger — the giant petrel is about the size of an albatross — and albatrosses are the largest, with a wingspan of up to 3.2 m. All of them have one thing in common: nostrils that are encased in a long "tube" to keep saltwater out of their noses when they dive.

Compared with other birds, tube-nosed birds have a particularly well developed sense of smell and it is likely that they use smell to locate food and breeding sites. Because they spend almost all of their lives at sea and are rarely able to drink freshwater, tube-nosed birds have the ability to excrete excess salt from their bodies through glands near their eyes. To feed their chicks, they store large quantities of a smelly, fishy oil in their stomachs. The oil is derived from the marine organisms they eat and parents later regurgitate it to feed offspring. Sometimes the thick, pungent oil is also squirted out in a bid to scare away predators.

Above: Shy Albatross (*Diomeda cauta*) and chick. *Below*: Wedge-tailed Shearwaters (*Puffinus pacificus*) feeding on a school of anchovies at Ningaloo Reef, Western Australia.

COLD-WEATHER WADDLERS

Penguins are extremely well adapted for life in freezing conditions. They cannot fly — therefore need no flight feathers — and their wings have evolved to become flippers, which are far more useful for their aquatic lifestyle. The fluffy feathers they do have are used to insulate penguins and keep them warm. Unlike the feathers of other birds, which are arranged in "tracts" over the body, the penguin's feathers provide even coverage. Beneath the feathers and the skin is a thick body covering of fat that traps heat in the penguin's body. Fat reserves also serve as food; when krill, fish and cephalopods are scarce, penguins simply live off their fat reserves.

Some penguin species spend almost three-quarters of their lives in the ocean, coming ashore only when they need to breed or moult. Although you wouldn't think stout penguins would be good jumpers, they are able to launch themselves as high as 1.8 m vertically from the ocean to an icy shelf to escape predators. Penguins must come onto land to moult, breed and lay eggs. Huddling together in large groups on the shore also helps penguins conserve their body heat. Sometimes, up to 60,000 penguins will squeeze into a tiny 16 ha area.

Penguins are ungainly waddlers on land, though streamlined swimmers in the water.

Young Little Penguins are covered in fluffy down to help protect them from the elements.

SURVIVING THE CHILL

Penguins endure temperature changes from −60°C in polar regions to 40°C at the equator. Those that live in polar regions must conserve heat while those that live in tropical areas have larger flippers and bare skin on the face that allows them to dissipate heat. Species that inhabit the sub-zero icy conditions of Antarctica incubate their eggs by sitting them on top of their feet and lifting the tips of their flippers up off the ice. In such chilly conditions, the eggs would freeze if left uncovered for even just a few seconds.

the FACTS!

THE BODY SHAPE of penguins has remained almost unchanged for at least 45 million years. They evolved from flying birds but later adapted to suit a life lived mostly in the water.

PENGUINS CAN SWIM very fast underwater — up to 40 km/h.

ONLY LITTLE PENGUINS (*Eudyptula minor*) nest on the Australian mainland. Others are found in the icy Antarctic Territory and on subantarctic islands.

PENGUINS ARE also excellent divers. Emperor Penguins (*Aptenodytes forsteri*), the largest penguin species, have been known to dive to as far as 565 m below the waves without seeming to be affected by water pressure.

YOUNG PENGUINS spend almost all of their first year at sea, feeding and growing fat. They begin to return to the colony when they are two years old.

BANDING STUDIES in Australia have shown that the longest-living penguin was 21 years old. Most penguins have an average lifespan of just five years.

Plunge-divers
— gannets & boobies

Masked Booby

the FACTS!

THE RED-FOOTED BOOBY (*Sula sula*) is Australia's smallest booby species and breeds only on islands off the Queensland coast.

BOTH SEXES OF BOOBY have similar plumage, with the exception of the Brown Booby (*Sula leucogaster*). The male Brown Booby has a blue mask, while the female's mask is yellow.

MALE GANNETS are larger than females but female boobies are larger than males.

BROWN BOOBIES (below) usually lay two or three eggs, but often only the first chick to hatch will survive. The first to hatch is the largest and strongest and is able to demand the biggest and best share of food.

BOOBY COMES from the Spanish, *bobo* (clown or fool) because sailors thought these birds were silly.

GANNETS are extremely swift dive-bombers and can dive from as high as 30 m above the water. They don't dive directly onto the fish, but rather below them and then shoot up and seize the fish from beneath.

Order: Pelecaniformes
Family: Sulidae

Diving seabirds such as gannets and boobies have air sacs just under the skin, which cushion the bird when it hits the water. They also have no external nostrils, so water cannot get up their noses when they dive.

THE WORLD'S THREE GANNET species live in temperate regions, while six booby species inhabit the tropics and subtropics. Four booby species and two gannet species are found in Australia.

Both gannets and boobies are sociable birds that form huge colonies where feeding, breeding and courting are carried out. Because of the amount of guano (bird droppings), these colonies are usually particularly smelly. Gannets and boobies are excellent deep-water divers and strike with precision to spear fish below the water's surface. Once a fish is caught, other members of the colony noisily demand their share of the spoils.

A colony of Australasian Gannets (*Morus serrator*) rests on a barren headland.

MASKED FACES

As well as similar slender, pointed wings and large bills, gannets and boobies share another common feature — their beaks fuse with their heads to form prominent facial "masks". Different species are distinguished by the colour of their face masks and feet. The mask alleviates the need for external nostrils and stops water from shooting up the bird's nose when it dives.

Right: These high-speed divers need a diving mask.

Below, left to right: A male Brown Booby; Masked Booby; Red-footed Booby.

Tropical soarers
— frigatebirds & tropicbirds

Order: Pelecaniformes
Families: Fregatidae & Phaethontidae

Frigatebirds and tropicbirds need a large wingspan to allow them to glide effortlessly over the oceans. They rely on winds and air currents to stay in the air because their large wings are not made for prolonged flapping; this seems strange for birds that spend almost all their lives in the air!

ALTHOUGH THEY LIVE A SIMILAR AIRBORNE LIFESTYLE to albatrosses, frigatebirds and tropicbirds prefer the warmth of the tropics and are not related. There are five species of frigatebird worldwide and three of them are found in Australia: the Great Frigatebird (*Fregata minor*), Lesser Frigatebird (*F. ariel*) and Christmas Frigatebird (*F. andrewsi*). Two tropicbird species, the Red-tailed Tropicbird (*Phaethon rubricauda*) and White-tailed Tropicbird (*P. lepturus*), soar over Australian waters.

Tropicbirds and frigatebirds have very different ways of obtaining food. Frigatebirds are the aerial pirates of the bird world, hijacking other species in mid-air and forcibly stealing their food. Flying-fish are also a favourite meal for frigatebirds. Tropicbirds prefer to soar 15–30 m above the water, swooping on flying-fish or, more often, plunge-diving for squid.

THERMAL HIGHS

Soaring seabirds take advantage of the updraught coming off the ocean's surface and thermal currents in the air to help them glide over the ocean. Gliding expends a lot less energy than flapping and seabirds could not afford to spend so much time in the air if they had to flap constantly to stay airborne. Instead, they glide in loops about 20–30 m above the waves. At this distance from the waves, the wind speed is no longer slowed by the friction of the ocean's surface and waves deflect air upwards to add "slope lift" to the air currents above. Seabirds can soar comfortably for 24 hours a day using the wind, waves and currents to help them save energy.

STREAMING SEABIRDS

Two long central tail feathers stream out behind tropicbirds as they fly; it is not known what purpose this serves. The Red-tailed Tropicbird (right and far right) is especially attractive. Its tail "streamers" are vivid scarlet and its plumage has a rosy pink flush. The Red-tailed Tropicbird nests on offshore islands in Australia's south-west and north-east. The White-tailed Tropicbird is rarely seen in Australia but sometimes visits north-eastern waters.

the FACTS!

FRIGATEBIRDS (above) do not have waterproof feathers, so they never deliberately land on the water's surface where they could become waterlogged.

ADULT MALE FRIGATEBIRDS are all black — only the Christmas Frigatebird and the Lesser Frigatebird have white on the ventral side. Females (below) are larger than males and all have white markings on the underside of their bodies.

FRIGATEBIRDS pair up for only one season but have a very long chick-rearing period. Young frigatebirds can fly at around 5–6 months but most keep returning to the nest to be fed until they are a year old.

TROPICBIRDS (left and below) spend their entire lives at sea and only return to land to breed. They even court each other in the air before landing and "pushing" themselves to the nest site because they are unable to walk well on their short legs.

Pelicans
— small bellies, big bills

Order: Pelecaniformes
Family: Pelecanidae

Dixon Merritt's limerick "A wonderful bird is the pelican, His bill will hold more than his belican" is quite correct — a pelican's beak can hold up to three times what it can fit in its stomach!

the FACTS!

ONE TO THREE EGGS are laid in each clutch and chicks are born featherless and helpless (above). Each chick consumes approximately 68 kg of fish before it is ready to leave the nest, by which time it has built up fat reserves to help it survive. Regardless, many pelican chicks die once they leave the nest.

PELICAN CHICKS at fledging weigh more than adults — this is because they have fat stores that help them survive until they can hunt successfully for themselves.

IN MEDIEVAL TIMES, people in Europe wrongly believed that pelicans used their long beaks to pierce their chests and feed their chicks on their own blood.

ADULT PELICANS do not vocalise (they are virtually voiceless). Instead, males court by posturing and display as the females fly overhead.

A FLOCK of these big-bodied flyers is collectively known as a "squadron".

ONCE THE PELICAN has a mouthful, water is filtered out of its enormous bill and any captured fish are turned around to be swallowed headfirst.

THE AUSTRALIAN PELICAN

(*Pelecanus conspicillatus*) is the world's largest pelican species. Fully grown adults can weigh as much as 7–8 kg. It also has the largest bill of any bird on the planet!

BIG-BILLED FISHERS

The huge pouch-like bill of Australian Pelicans can attain a maximum length of 50 cm and enables the pelican to swallow fish that are as much as 30 cm long! Each bird eats around 2 kg of fish every day. Pelicans will also scoop up tadpoles, frogs, crabs and sometimes even turtles.

Australian Pelicans are the continent's largest flying seabird species. They can have a body length of 1.8 m and a wingspan of up to 3.4 m.

FLYING & FLOCKING

Pelicans belong to the same order as frigatebirds and albatrosses, and similarly use thermal air currents to help them circle up to 3 km above the surface of the sea. In spite of their size, they are capable flyers and are able to make long-distance flights if necessary. Pelicans frequently form loose flocks of hundreds of birds and fly in V-shaped formation.

BREEDING & NESTING

Pelicans also form crowded, noisy breeding colonies, often on inland lakes or watercourses. Elaborate dances and courtship displays include fluttering their pouches (which change colour during breeding season), strutting, flying and swimming in circles. Females scrape out a shallow nest on the ground and lay 1–3 eggs (incubated by both parents).

Below: Pelicans sometimes cooperate in order to catch fish. To do this, they form tight circles and "herd" the fish into a group before scooping them up.

Divers & spearers
— cormorants & Darter

Order: Pelecaniformes
Family: Anhingidae & Phalacrocoracidae

Rivers, estuaries and coastal watercourses across much of the mainland are prime habitat for these long-necked fishers that some people call "shags".

ONLY ONE OF THE WORLD'S four darter species, *Anhinga melanogaster*, is found in Australia, which is also home to five cormorant species — the Little Pied (*Phalacrocorax melanoleucos*), Black-faced (*P. fuscescens*), Pied (*P. varius*, above right), Little Black (*P. sulcirostris*) and Great Cormorant (*P. carbo*).

IN PURSUIT OF PREY

Australia's Darter and cormorant species may look similar, both with long necks and webbed feet for propulsion underwater, but they employ different tactics for catching a meal. The Darter slips steathily into the water and waits, with its snake-like neck above the water, until fish, frogs or turtles swim under the shadow of its outstretched wings and tail. It then draws back its S-shaped neck and, with its pointed beak partly open, quickly spears its prey. When it returns to the surface, the Darter tosses its prey upwards and swallows it headfirst. Streamlined cormorants chase and catch their prey underwater before returning to the surface to swallow the meal headfirst.

DRYING OUT

Despite spending a large part of their lives in the water, cormorants and darters do not have waterproof feathers. This lack of waterproofing allows water to permeate their feathers, making it easier for them to slip into and under the water. However, they must be careful that their absorbent feathers do not become waterlogged. Before flying, darters and cormorants must leave the water and dry out by spreading their wings wide in the sun.

Top to bottom: Little Pied Cormorants nest in colonies; The snake-like neck of the Darter; A Darter dries its wings in the sun.

the FACTS!

SOMETIMES THE DARTER is known as the "Snake-bird" because of its habit of swimming with just its head and neck out of the water.

DARTERS FREQUENTLY build their stick nests on branches that overhang the water.

SOME FISHERMEN IN ASIA keep flocks of trained cormorants to help them catch fish. They tie a collar on the cormorant to prevent it devouring the fish and attach it to a line or leash so the bird can dive. When the bird resurfaces, they pull it to the boat and steal its fish.

THE GREAT CORMORANT (below) uses the same nest each year but adds to it. The pile of sticks that makes up a Great Cormorant's nest can be as much as 2 m thick.

CORMORANT POO, or guano, is mined for fertiliser in some parts of the world.

FOSSILS found in Central Australia indicate that ancient birds similar to cormorants lived around 20 million years ago in Australia's inland sea.

THE GALAPAGOS CORMORANT, (*Nannopterum harrisi*) cannot fly. It jumps into the water and scrambles up rock ledges to get out.

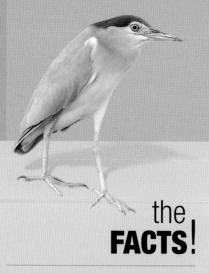

Elegant hunters
— herons, bitterns & egrets

Order: Ciconiiformes
Family: Ardeidae

Characteristic long legs and long necks enable these wading waterbirds to stalk the shallows hunting for prey.

the FACTS!

DURING BREEDING SEASON, bitterns are particularly noisy and make some of the loudest sounds of all birds. The booming breeding calls of the Australasian Bittern can sometimes be heard from more than 1 km away!

ROAST BITTERNS were a favourite dinner dish for England's King Henry VIII in the Middle Ages.

THE WHITE-NECKED HERON (*Ardea pacifica*) is endemic to Australia, but some stray individuals have been recorded as far away as New Zealand and New Guinea.

EGRETS AND HERONS are actually the same sort of bird! All belong to the genera *Ardea* and *Egretta*, but generally white species are called egrets and those with coloured plumage are known as herons.

WHEN IT RAINS, some heron species protect their chicks by standing above the nest with their wings outspread.

WHITE-FACED HERONS (*Egretta novaehollandiae*) are the most common Australian herons.

Above: The Great Egret (*Ardea alba*) is the largest egret. Its long breeding plumes were once popular for ladies' hats, which led to wholesale slaughter of this species.

HERONS AND EGRETS are graceful waders that inhabit Australia's coastal and inland waterways and wetlands, where they nest and breed in large colonies. Although herons and egrets are quite beautiful in form, their voices are anything but! They are all unable to sing; instead, their colonies resound with loud croaking calls and groans. The call of one of the rarest species, the Great-billed Heron (*Ardea sumatrana*) of north Australia, is sometimes likened to the roar of a bull.

Bitterns share the heron's watery habitat, but are smaller, shyer reed-dwellers. Three bittern species, out of the twelve global species, live in Australia. Dull plumage allows bitterns to camouflage themselves among the reeds, where they stand extremely still with their long necks and bills pointed skywards and sway from side to side when the wind moves the reeds and rushes.

WADERS IN THE NIGHT

Nine heron species worldwide are known as night herons because they are nocturnal hunters. Night herons are also stockier and smaller than most other herons. Australia has just one night heron species, the Rufous (Nankeen) Night Heron (*Nycticorax caledonicus,* left). During the day, colonies of Rufous Night Herons roost in the tree tops before flying to hunting grounds at twilight to feed. They are a colourful species with "rufous" or chestnut plumage on the back, cream on the belly, and blue-black heads.

Below: A flock of egrets feasts on an aquatic smorgasbord at Fogg Dam in the Northern Territory.

Long necks & bills
— spoonbills, storks & ibises

Conservation Watch
The Black-necked Stork is rare in the southern area of its range, although it is relatively common in northern coastal areas.

Order: Ciconiiformes
Families: Ciconiidae & Threskiornithidae

SCOOPING SPOONBILLS

Few people would think that spoonbills and ibises are closely related, but they both belong to the same family and have similar lifestyles. Australia has two species of spoonbill, the Yellow-billed Spoonbill (*Platalea flavipes*) and the Royal Spoonbill (*P. regia*) — both are nomadic and travel along waterways moving their heads backwards and forwards in the water to capture insects, small fish, crustaceans and molluscs in the deep spoon at the base of their bills. Spoonbills' beaks are lined with extremely sensitive nerve endings, which help the bird detect vibrations in the water to find prey. Spoonbills sometimes consume hundreds of aquatic animals per day.

The Yellow-billed Spoonbill is only found on Australia's mainland. Males have longer bills than females.

ONE OF A KIND

Only one stork species is found in Australia — the Black-necked Stork (*Ephippiorhynchus asiaticus*), or Jabiru as it is also known. It is distinguished from other wading birds by its glossy black beak and bright red legs. Black-necked Storks creep up on prey but often have to run and hop, with their wings flapping, to catch their meal. Like all storks they lack muscles in their syrinx that would allow them to call and are largely mute, although they do make clacking sounds with their beaks when nesting.

A snake is on the menu for this female Black-necked Stork. They are opportunistic carnivores and also eat crustaceans, fish, insects, frogs and rodents.

PECKING FARMHANDS

Australia has three species of ibis — the Australian White Ibis (*Threskiornis molucca*), Straw-necked Ibis (*T. spinicollis*) and Glossy Ibis (*Plegadis falcinellus*). All species live in colonies and flock together. White Ibis flocks, especially, can be enormous, with more than 10,000 birds recorded gathering in one place in Victoria. Like Cattle Egrets (*Ardea ibis*) — which were introduced in 1933 to help keep cattle free from ticks and parasites — ibises can be a big help for farmers. Crop farmers especially welcome ibises because they help keep Australia's crops free from pests such as grasshoppers, locusts and plagues of mice. When a flock of ibises forages through crops, each ibis is able to eat about 25% of its own body weight in invertebrates every day!

the FACTS!

WHEN COURTING, the male spoonbill tries to nibble at the female's bill while she resists by bobbing her head up and down. When she finally relents and lets him nibble her bill, the match is made and the two will mate. Male Yellow-billed Spoonbills can be very aggressive with other males during the breeding season.

MALE AND FEMALE Black-necked Storks (below) can be distinguished by their eye colour. Males have black eyes while the female's eyes are bright yellow.

BLACK-NECKED STORKS use their beaks and throats to carry water to their chicks.

THE IBIS is significant to South Australia's Kaurna Aborigines whose creation ancestor, Tjilbruke, transformed into a Glossy Ibis following the death of his nephew.

THERE ARE 26 IBIS SPECIES worldwide, yet ibises have more endangered species than any other type of wading bird.

THE STRAW-NECKED IBIS is found only in Australia. It takes its name from the stiff, scruffy yellowish feathers on the front of its neck.

Dancers & nomads
— Brolgas, cranes & bustards

Order: Gruiformes
Families: Gruidae & Otididae

After the Emu and cassowary, beautiful elegant cranes and the shy, plains-wandering Australian Bustard are among the continent's tallest bird species.

AUSTRALIA HAS TWO BEAUTIFUL crane species — the Brolga (*Grus rubicunda*) and the Sarus Crane (*G. antigone*). They were believed to be the same species until ornithologists recognised that the Sarus Crane's red facial plumage continued further down its neck and it lacked the Brolga's black-feathered "dewlap" under the chin. The Brolga is most famous for its spectacular dancing. During the dry season, large flocks of Brolgas congregate at Kakadu and other permanent wetlands in north Australia. They greet each other with a graceful ceremonial dance of bowing with their wings outstretched, and leaping up and down. Brolgas and cranes live, breed and feed in shallow wetlands and swamps, where they eat the fleshy stems of water plants, reeds, tubers and seeds. Occasionally they will prise open the shells of some snails and molluscs.

The beautiful silvery-grey Brolga can stand up to 1.3 m tall and has a wingspan of up to 2.4 m.

the FACTS!

THE BROLGA (below) was thought to be Australia's only crane species until the Sarus Crane was recognised in 1966.

BOTH THE MALE AND FEMALE brolga incubate the eggs, which are laid into a shallow nest of dry grass or sedges that is scraped together to form a mound (left) in shallow swamplands.

BROLGA CHICKS can run and swim just a few hours after hatching but it takes around 100 days for them to grow flight feathers and start to learn to fly.

UNLIKE OTHER WADERS (such as herons), cranes do not have breeding plumage. Instead, they dance to attract a mate.

AUSTRALIAN BUSTARDS are usually silent, but during mating season they attract females with a loud "booming" call that has been likened to the distant roar of a lion.

OUTBACK NOMADS

Reclusive Australian Bustards are nomadic plains-dwellers that prefer to walk rather than fly. However, they can fly if threatened and are the continent's heaviest flying birds. Males may weigh as much as 12 kg, although most grow only to about 7.5 kg. Females are slightly smaller at around 4 kg. Bustards have a surprising system of attracting a mate. Males gather in groups (known as "leks") of about ten individuals and fluff up the feathers on their necks to resemble feather boas (left). Females then assess the males, choosing the one they think displays the best. During the breeding season, males spend much of their time displaying and little time feeding; by the end of it, most males are extremely thin.

Water-walkers
— swamphens, rails & coots

Order: Gruiformes
Family: Rallidae

Swift little members of the Rallidae family live, nest and feed near water. They have small bodies with short wings and tails, long legs and toes that allow them to quickly scoot over the water's surface.

SWAMPHENS AND COOTS are familiar visitors to ponds, wetlands and lakes around the continent, where they forage in the water and at the water's edge for insects, frogs and aquatic vegetation. Flying may not appear to be the strongest skill of crakes, rails, swamphens and coots, but many species are actually nomadic and make long migrations to their preferred habitats. Some species, such as the Eurasian Coot, can be prolific in an area one day and almost absent days later when the flock moves on. The few species that are largely flightless are light enough and quick enough to speedily swim or run off if threatened. Many can dive underwater for some time as a defence strategy.

M & I MORCOMBE

the FACTS!

THE PURPLE SWAMPHEN (above) lives in small, communal family groups of 2–7 males with a few females. They practise polygamy (having more than one female partner) and polyandry (more than one male partner). All members of the group help build nesting platforms by trampling down reeds and vegetation and all take turns brooding the eggs.

SWAMPHENS can be carnivorous and will chase and eat ducklings and the chicks of other waterbirds.

THE TASMANIAN NATIVE-HEN is a very weak flyer and prefers to run or swim to escape danger. Surprisingly, it can run at a speed of up to 48 km/h!

CRAKES are some of the rarest members of the Rallidae family. Australia has six crake species.

EURASIAN COOTS are nomadic birds that flock together and make noisy "kyok" sounds as well as harsh screeches.

BUFF-BANDED RAILS hoard food to eat later.

BIG FAMILY

Australia has seventeen species in this widespread family. The most common is the glossy Purple Swamphen. Other species, such as the Buff-banded Rail and crakes, have beautiful spotted plumage that allows them to hide among reeds and grasses. Less commonly seen are Lewin's Rail (*Rallus pectoralis*), the Red-necked Crake (*Rallina tricolor*), which inhabits only a small territory in Cape York, and the mangrove-dwelling Chestnut Rail (*Eulabeornis castaneoventris*).

Clockwise from top left: Purple Swamphen (*Porphyrio porhyrio*); The Tasmanian Native-hen (*Gallinula mortierii*) once existed on the mainland but suffered from predation (probably by Dingoes); Female Buff-banded Rail (*Gallirallus philippensis*); Male Buff-banded Rail.

Below: A Eurasian Coot (*Fulica atra*) darts across the water's surface.

BELOW LEFT: M & I MORCOMBE

Black-fronted Dotterel

Oddball waders
— dotterels, plovers & relatives

Order: Charadriiformes **Families:** Rostratulidae, Jacanidae, Burhinidae, Haematopodidae, Recurvirostridae, Charadriidae & Glareolidae

Almost 10% of Australia's bird species belong to this order of small to medium-sized waders and shorebirds. Each has specialised adaptations to suit its diet and habitat.

the FACTS!

THE PAINTED SNIPE is native to Australia. Although it looks like a snipe, it is probably more closely related to jacanas.

STONE-CURLEWS are sometimes called "thick-knees" because of the prominent joints on their legs.

FEMALE COMB-CRESTED JACANAS (*Metopidius gallinacea*) may mate with up to five males, who then look after her eggs while she goes off in search of another partner.

MALE COMB-CRESTED JACANAS sit on the eggs and look after the chicks for 2–3 weeks after they hatch. If danger threatens, the chicks sometimes climb under the father's wing and he carries them away to safety.

COMB-CRESTED JACANAS are also known as Lilytrotters because they carefully trot over lily pads.

THE BANDED STILT (*Cladorhynchus leucocephalus*) is found only in Australia. It somehow knows when inland lakes are flooded and moves from the coast to the lakes to feed on shrimps and breed. However, if the water dries up again before hatchlings can fly, the parents abandon them.

WHEN THE Black-winged Stilt (left) flies, its extremely long legs trail out behind its body.

AUSTRALIA HAS A WEALTH of wading birds, both native to this country and visitors from as far afield as Mongolia and Siberia. Some, such as the Black-fronted Dotterel (*Elseyornis melanops*), Inland Dotterel (*Charadrius australis*) and pratincoles, prefer freshwater inland habitats, while others, such as pharalopes, the Red-capped Plover (*C. ruficapillus*) and two sand plover species, prefer the coast. Although they share habitat, species reduce competition by focusing on a particular food source. Stilts and avocets use their long, slender bills to snatch up shrimps and marine organisms, while oystercatchers have a thicker, sharper beak to poke into the shells of molluscs and crustaceans.

NIGHT HUNTERS

Stone-curlews are waders that feed at night either on dry land (Bush Stone-curlew) or the beach (Beach Stone-curlew). By day, their speckled plumage helps them camouflage and they often lie flat on the ground or stand stock still in bushland with their heads tucked close to their shoulders to avoid detection. However, if they are protecting chicks, they fan their wings, rush forwards and hiss threats. Because they need to see in the dark, stone-curlews have larger eyes than most other waders. They stay still and silent by day and at night let out an eerie, spine-tingling wailing. They feed by moonlight on crustaceans, small reptiles, mammals, insects and some plant matter.

Right, top to bottom: Bush Stone-curlews (*Burhinus grallarius*) dance and sing a series of whistles and shrieks when breeding. *Below*: Comb-crested Jacanas have vivid scarlet combs that fade to a duller yellow when an individual feels submissive.

M & I MORCOMBE

BLUFF & FLUFF

Most waders and shorebirds construct basic nests that are often little more than a scrape in the ground. They use different ruses to lure predators away from the nest or vulnerable hatchlings. The Painted Snipe (*Rostratula benghalensis*) will "freeze" if disturbed, hoping to convince the intruder it is a piece of the scenery.

If the threat remains, the bird fans out its wings, fluffs up its feathers and tail in an attempt to look bigger, and hisses at the intruder. Red-capped Plovers lie flat on the ground, dragging their spread-out wings along as if broken. Both male and female Black-winged Stilts brood and rear their chicks. To protect them, the parents will feign injury and may also yap, chorus or flap around acrobatically.

the FACTS!

THE BANDED LAPWING (*Vanellus tricolor*, below), is found only in Australia. It is often seen pecking among ploughed land and mown grasses near agricultural areas.

YOUNG OYSTERCATCHERS have to learn how to prise open shells — it is not an innate ability. Researchers have discovered that some oystercatchers knock limpets off rocks to get into them, while others prise them open with their beaks. Individuals never use a combination of these techniques. The difference appears to be how the birds were taught to do the task by their parents.

BEACH STONE-CURLEWS (*Esacus neglectus*, below) are not as nocturnal as their Bush Stone-curlew relatives, but still usually rest in the shade by day. They wade the coastal intertidal zone or sandy flats near mangroves searching for crabs and marine invertebrates.

Clockwise from top: Australian Pratincole; Red-necked Phalarope; Inland Dotterel.

COAST TO CREEK

A few birds that are considered waders spend their lives inland. The plains and claypans of inland Australia attract the Australian Pratincole (*Stiltia isabella*), which, unlike most waders, catches some of its food in flight. Before inland storms, many thousands of these birds gather in flocks and fly en masse in acrobatic displays. Arid and semi-arid inlands are also habitat for the small Inland Dotterel, which feeds on succulent plants and insects and breeds when it rains. In contrast, phalaropes are true aquatic waders that spend most of their lives at sea, floating in shallow water to peck up krill and shrimps. As they feed, they spin around in circles, creating a whirlpool effect to stir up food from below.

SHELL OPENERS

Oystercatchers, with their red legs and red-orange bills, are among the most commonly seen shorebirds. They use their sharp, stabbing beaks to feed on hard-shelled molluscs such as pipis, limpets and oysters, which they crack open or chisel off the rocks. To open bivalves, they peck away at the muscle that holds the shell closed to get to the meaty shellfish.

Right: A Pied Oystercatcher uses its long, thin beak to prise open a pipi.

AUSTRALIAN PRATINCOLES live in the dry interior where they sometimes build a nest of rabbit poo! When the chicks hatch, they may also creep into the shelter of a rabbit burrow if danger lurks.

Long-haul visitors
— migratory waders

Order: Charadriiformes & Procellariiformes
Families: Recurvirostridae, Procellariidae & Scolopacidae

Making the most of the Earth's habitats is no problem for some long-distance species that may fly as much as 16,800 km from their homeland to feeding and breeding grounds in Australia.

the FACTS!

STINTS, such as the Red-necked Stint (*Calidris ruficollis*, above), are some of the smallest migratory birds (12–16 cm high), but that did not stop one Red-necked Stint from flying 12,494 km on a one-way trip!

RESEARCH CARRIED OUT by the Australian Bird and Bat Banding Scheme found that the species that made the longest one-way migration was the Arctic Tern (of the family Laridae), which travelled 16,776 km from where it was banded. Arctic Terns fly from the Arctic to the Antarctic each year.

ALONG WITH INSTINCT it is thought that migratory birds use the positions of the sun and stars, or the Earth's magnetic field, to help them navigate.

SOME SMALL MIGRATORY species almost double their body weight before setting off for a long flight. The extra fat reserves provide them with fuel on journeys where they may not stop for 5000 km.

AUSTRALIA HAS AN ABUNDANCE of seasonally wet habitats. At certain times of the year wetlands, such as the Coorong in South Australia, can become crowded with an influx of hundreds of thousands of migratory birds. Every year, as many as 33 bird species may settle temporarily on this 47,000 ha area.

AROUND 69 BIRD SPECIES are recorded visitors to Australian shores. Stints, sandpipers, greenshanks and godwits, together with Red Knots and turnstones are some of the world's most mobile species. These long-distance specialists may cover 10,000 km on each migration.

How migratory birds manage to migrate around the globe is still being studied; however, for many migratory species the flight path is entirely instinctive. Adult Short-tailed Shearwaters, for instance, abandon their fat, fluffy chicks and fly home alone; however, when the chicks are old enough, they will instinctively fly to the adults' breeding grounds.

In early August, after a long journey from northern Asia, thousands of Black-tailed Godwits (*Limosa limosa*) descend on the Gulf and coast of Arnhem Land, where they will feed until their return flight in March or April. Annual visitors to Western Australia's Roebuck Bay include up to 100,000 Bar-tailed Godwits (*L. lapponica*). Three snipe species also fly in from their Japanese or Russian breeding grounds to feast on seeds and invertebrates in freshwater or brackish swamps along Australia's eastern coast.

Below: Bar-tailed Godwits fly to Australia in August each year. Most return to Northern Hemisphere breeding grounds in April and May, but some young birds remain here all year.

Conservation Watch

Populations of Black-tailed Godwits (left) are declining rapidly in some areas and it has now been listed as near threatened by the IUCN Red List.

Above, left to right: The Bar-tailed Godwit's long beak is used to hunt marine molluscs; Common Sandpipers are often seen perching on boats; Ruddy Turnstones turn over stones to find food.

SKY-HIGH FLYWAYS

Migrating birds fly along a number of regular routes that criss-cross the globe and are known as "flyways". Most flyways take the birds over regular feeding and resting grounds, so it is extremely important that these stop-over points are preserved. The East Asian–Australasian Flyway is one of the most threatened flyways. It usually takes birds from Siberia and Alaska in the Arctic Circle through northern and South-East Asia to Australia and New Zealand — on this flight path, birds may fly over as many as twenty countries!

Usually birds stop and recuperate up to four times on their journey, mostly on tidal mudflats or beaches, where flocks of many different species often gather, mustering up the energy to continue on their journey. Destruction of just some of these rest stops could have a devastating impact on migratory species because it may mean that one leg of the journey becomes too long for the birds to fly.

International conventions such as RAMSAR, which protects wetlands, have been established to protect migratory waders' habitat and resting areas. Vitally important Australian sites are Eighty Mile Beach and Roebuck Bay in Western Australia (where up to 300,000 birds gather each year), as well as Kakadu and the Gulf of Carpentaria, from where newly arrived bird species spread south or to inland lakes in the continent's interior.

the FACTS!

AGREEMENTS such as the Japan Australia Migratory Birds Agreement (JAMBA) and its Chinese equivalent CAMBA help protect species.

APPROXIMATELY 2–3 MILLION birds migrate to Australia each year.

MOST MIGRATORY BIRD species fly at a height of less than 91 m from the ground or ocean.

OVER THEIR LIFETIME, some migratory waders fly further than the distance between Earth and the moon!

IN PARTS OF ASIA, some wading birds are a traditional food source and as many as 1.5 million may end up on dinner plates each year.

BANDING STUDIES allow researchers to figure out how many birds migrate to Australia, what types of birds they are and how far they have flown. However, it requires that the birds are caught twice — once to band them and then again to check them — which is not always an easy feat!

THE LARGEST MIGRANT WADER in the world is the 65 cm tall Eastern Curlew (*Numenius madagascariensis*, below), which travels to Australia from icy Siberia and Mongolia.

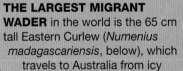

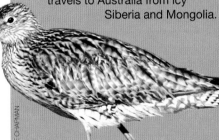

Above: Migratory waders sometimes form huge flocks of many thousands of birds.

Sea hunters
— gulls, terns & relatives

Order: Charadriiformes
Family: Laridae

Few trips to the beach are complete without a flock of squawking, hungry gulls squabbling to scavenge fish and chips. At certain times of year they share their scavenging lifestyles with long-distance visitors such as skuas, terns and jaegers, many of which breed in polar regions.

GLOBALLY, there are around 45 gull species and 42 tern species, but only three gull species and fourteen tern species breed in Australia. Other gull and tern species occasionally visit, along with skuas and their slightly smaller relatives, the jaegers. Australian waters are frequented by two skua species, the South Polar Skua (*Catharacta maccormicki*) and the Great Skua (*C. skua*); both breed on Antarctic Islands. Migrating to Australia from the Arctic circle are three jaegar species — the Arctic (*Stercorarius parasiticus*), Pomarine (*S. pomarinus*) and Long-tailed (*S. longicuadus*).

Below: A band of black on the back of the neck distinguishes the Black-naped Tern (*Sterna sumatrana*).

the FACTS!

THE PACIFIC GULL (*Larus pacificus*, above) is a native Australian species. It is one of the largest gulls in the world and can grow up to 66 cm long. There are two races of the Pacific Gull — the race *georgii* has red eyes, distinguishing it from the white-eyed *pacificus* race.

THE KELP GULL (*Larus dominicanus*) was first recorded in Australia in 1943 but has since become common along parts of the east coast.

SILVER GULLS (*Larus novaehollandiae*, below) were some of the first participants in scientific studies of bird behaviour that earned Dutch zoologist Nico Tinbergen a Nobel Prize.

GARBAGE-GUT GULLS

Only one gull species, the Pacific Gull, is endemic to Australia, but it is much less common than the ubiquitous Silver Gull, which goes just about anywhere and eats just about anything! Gulls' natural diet of fish, crustaceans and marine organisms is frequently supplemented by human rubbish and food scavenged from campsites and picnic tables. Such resourcefulness has allowed this species to become widespread.

Conservation Watch

Most species of Australian gull, tern, skua, jaeger and noddy are common and secure. Some, such as the Caspian Tern (left), are less commonly seen because their populations fluctuate seasonally.

A flock of Silver Gulls descend upon the remains of an Australian Fur-seal attacked by a White Shark off the coast of southern Australia. Ever the opportunist, this familiar bird manages to find a meal in almost every Australian environment.

RON & VALERIE TAYLOR

CHICK-GOBBLING HUNTERS

Skuas and jaegars are fast-flying predatory carnivores with sharply curved beaks that they use to peck and harass smaller seabirds, such as prions and storm-petrels, to steal their catch. Usually, they chase the birds in the air and snatch up the disgorged meal in mid-flight. If the birds refuse to release their meal, skuas and jaegars will devour the birds instead. On rare occasions they dive down to catch their own fish. Jaegers and skuas are also partial to seabird eggs and chicks.

TAKE YOUR TERN

Slender, graceful terns are smaller than gulls and are fishers rather than scavengers. Terns will also catch and eat insects while flying, and some inland species exist on a diet of small terrestrial vertebrates. Living and nesting in huge, noisy colonies helps terns to protect themselves from predators. Most species lay one to three eggs per clutch and pairs share the domestic duties of nest building and raising chicks, with both the male and female taking a turn.

Common, Lesser and Black Noddies (left) are terns that live in subtropical or tropical regions. Coral cays often become large breeding colonies for these noisy and sociable seabirds. Both parents help to build a nest of leaves, seaweed and vegetation either on top of a low shrub or on the ground. All three species lay just one egg and both parents incubate the egg for around 35 days. Noddies are such committed parents that when brooding they are extremely reluctant to leave the nest. During the breeding season they remain on the nest — even if humans approach closely — and can easily be caught by hand.

the FACTS!

SOOTY TERNS (*Sterna fuscata*) spend much of their early life at sea, only returning to land when they begin to breed at around four years of age.

FLOCKS OF COMMON NODDIES (*Anous stolidus*), known as "rafts", sometimes communally hunt shoals of fish far out to sea.

CRESTED TERNS (*Sterna bergii*), like other terns, mirror each other's flight when courting, gracefully flying together wing tip to wing tip and spiralling up in the air.

THE WHITE TERN (*Gygis alba*) does not build a nest. Instead, females lay a single egg in a fork, notch or depression on a tree branch.

AN ARCTIC TERN (*Sterna paradisaea*) can cover as much as 32,000 km in a year.

ARCTIC TERNS keep the same partners and nest sites, laying their eggs directly onto the ground. The eggs are speckled to help them blend in with the rocks and gravel.

SOOTY TERNS can spend up to three years in the air without landing!

Bridled Tern (*Sterna anaethetus*)

Modern-day dodos
— pigeons & doves

Order: Columbiformes
Family: Columbidae

It may not look like a pigeon, but DNA evidence proves that the flightless extinct Dodo of Mauritius belongs to the same bird family as doves and pigeons. Australia has 25 species of these plump, cooing birds, and 23 of them are native to this continent.

the FACTS!

THE DODO (above) became extinct in 1680. It was killed by Portuguese and Dutch sailors and introduced pests such as pigs and monkeys destroyed its habitat.

THE DIAMOND DOVE (*Geopelia cuneata*, below) is Australia's smallest dove.

PIGEONS ARE UNIQUE in feeding their young pigeon-milk, which is derived from the breakdown of some of the parent's own internal cells. Pigeon-milk is nutritious with a high fat content.

SURGEON BENJAMIN BYNOE collected the first specimen of a Spinifex Pigeon in 1839 on the Victoria River, Northern Territory.

THE WONGA PIGEON (*Leucosarcia melanoleuca*, below) was highly prized by early settlers for its meat and its numbers decreased considerably.

DOVES AND PIGEONS all belong to the same family. The difference in name is solely due to size, with most smaller species being called doves and larger ones, pigeons. Pigeons and doves share a few physiological differences from most other birds. Instead of tipping their heads back to drink, pigeons use their beaks like a straw to suck up water. They feed their young a regurgitated secretion called pigeon-milk, which is made up of water and broken-down food mixed in the crop, and their feathers also fall out more easily than the feathers of most other species, which is probably a defence mechanism. In Australia, members of this diverse family occupy a variety of habitats from rainforest to semi-arid spinifex grasslands.

The Pied Imperial-Pigeon (*Ducula bicolor*) nests on islands off the coast of north Australia.

CRESTS, PLUMES & TOPKNOTS

Some pigeon species are easily recognised by their prominent head wear. Unlike cockatoos, pigeons and doves are unable to raise or lower their crests. The Spinifex Pigeon (*Geophaps plumifera*) is an unmistakeable resident of rocky and sandy spinifex country and is sometimes called the Plumed Pigeon. It lives in flocks and searches the stone country for insects, grubs and grass seeds. Similar to the Spinifex Pigeon, but lacking the bright red eye patch and red-orange colouring with white bands, is the pretty pink-grey Crested Pigeon (*Ocyphaps lophotes*). The Topknot Pigeon (*Lopholaimus antarcticus*) is unique among the world's pigeon species and has no close relatives.

Below, left to right: Spinifex Pigeon; Topknot Pigeon; Crested Pigeon.

BRIGHT, SHINY THINGS

Iridescence, speckled feathers, barred feathers and brilliantly coloured plumage are found in a number of Australian dove and pigeon species and help these birds blend in with their preferred habitats. Fruit-loving rainforest doves, although resplendent with colour, are often hard to make out in the rainforest canopy, where their colours can be mistaken for the fruit and flowers of rainforest vegetation. Even some of the duller pigeons and doves may have intricate facial stripes, spotted breasts and a range of colours. The Common Bronzewing is the most widespread native species. Its plumage is anything but dull, with iridescent speckling on the wing tips and blue, dusky mauve and yellow tones decorating the neck and head.

The Superb Fruit-Dove (*Ptilinopus superbus*) is surprisingly hard to see in the forest canopy.

The most widespread native pigeon is the Common Bronzewing (*Phaps chalcoptera*).

SEED SOWERS

Fruit-dove species in the genera *Ptilinopus*, *Ducula* and *Lopholaimus* are vitally important to the health of the continent's rainforest and monsoon vine forest habitats. These fruit-eaters act as avian distributers of seeds for lilly-pillies and fruiting plants such as the Blue Quandong. Fleshy parts of the fruit are digested by the birds, but the hard seeds pass out with the birds' waste and are thus distributed throughout the birds' range.

Left: Wompoo Fruit-Doves (*Ptilinopus magnificus*) often hang upside down from branches to get at ripe fruit and berries. *Right*: The pretty, pastel Rose-crowned Fruit-Dove (*Ptilinopus regina*) breeds during the wet season, laying a single egg.

the FACTS!

THE PIGEONS that are most often seen gathering on monuments and statues in our public squares are actually the introduced Feral Pigeon (*Columba livia*). Feral Pigeons were first domesticated 3000 years ago, and have been used as messengers for many hundreds of years. Australia's Feral Pigeons most likely came over with the First Fleet.

IN WORLD WAR II allied forces considered using carrier pigeons to drop bombs on the enemy.

THE CHESTNUT-QUILLED Rock-Pigeon (*Petrophassa rufipennis*, below) has a limited habitat in the sandstone escarpments of the Top End, but is locally common within its range. It is named for the brilliant bands of bright chestnut on its extended wings.

THE MOST abundant bird species in the world was the North American Passenger Pigeon. In 1808 it was estimated that a single flock contained 2000 million birds! Humans hunted the birds mercilessly and in 1914 the last Passenger Pigeon died in Cincinnatti Zoo, America.

Cockatoos
— clever characters

Order: Psittaciformes
Family: Cacatuidae

Cockatoos are genetically different from other parrots and hence belong to the family Cacatuidae. They are the only parrots able to move their crests and their brightly plumed headgear is often used to convey moods and signal interest or threat.

the FACTS!

AUSTRALIA'S SMALLEST
cockatoo species is the grey, yellow and white, red-cheeked Cockatiel (*Nymphicus hollandicus*, above), which is sometimes called the Quarrion or Weero because of the sound of its call.

GALAHS (*Cacatua roseicapilla*) have been observed playing in whirlwinds — deliberately letting themselves be sucked up into the wind tunnel and spiralling upwards, only to repeat the process once they are blown out the top.

THE LARGEST SPECIES is the Palm Cockatoo (*Probisciger alterrimus*, below). The Palm Cockatoo has an unusual courtship routine. Males use their dextrous zygodactylus toes to grasp a chunk of wood and bang it against their perch, making a resonant drumming that can carry for several kilometres.

QUENCHING A THIRST

All cockatoos require water daily and usually descend upon waterholes in a large flock at dawn. This limits their habitats to places where water can be found within a 1–2 hour flight. Explorer Ludwig Leichhardt knew this and used it to find water for his expedition party by following a flock of corellas. Many people have been lucky enough to see the amusing antics of Galahs when it rains. Galahs inhabit hot, dusty areas of the continent, where little rain ever falls; when it does, it is little wonder these birds carry on like the proverbial "flamin' galah". Their inane behaviour includes swinging upside down with wings spread akimbo to allow the rain to penetrate to their inner feathers, flush out parasites and give them a good soak.

Right: Galahs tear away the bark around the entrance to their nesting hollows, which only serves to make their nests more obvious. It has been suggested they do this to impede the climbing ability of monitor lizards, which devour bird eggs.

Above: Major Mitchell's Cockatoo (*Cacatua leadbeateri*) was eventually named after Sir Thomas Mitchell who illustrated it in his 1838 book *Three Expeditions into the Interior of Eastern Australia*. It was first described in 1831 and originally named Leadbeater's Cockatoo.

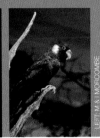

Conservation Watch

Glossy Black-Cockatoos (*Calyptorhynchus lathami*) are endangered, as are the Short-billed Black-Cockatoo (*C. latirostris*) and the Victorian race of the Red-tailed Black-Cockatoo (*C. banksii graptogyne*).

COPYCAT COCKIES

It is a well-known fact that cockatoos are excellent mimics when in captivity. What is little known is why they do this when they do not exhibit mimicry in the wild. It is thought that a high level of intelligence and a naturally sociable lifestyle makes cockies mimic humans when in captivity in order to improve their relationship. Research from the Netherlands' University of Leiden suggests that parrots may be such adept mimics because they are able to manipulate their tongues to make certain sounds. Sulphur-crested Cockatoos (*Cacatua galerita*) live for up to 30 years in the wild and even longer in captivity. They are highly intelligent and have excellent memories, so they can easily memorise words.

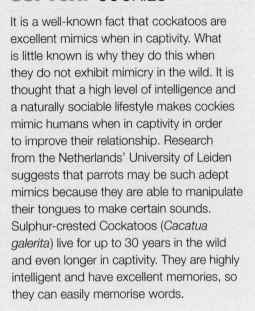

the FACTS!

A LITTLE CORELLA (*Cacatua sanguinea*, above) is the oldest wild parrot recorded in Australia so far. It was tagged in 1901 and later found dead on the road in 1972, making it 71 years old.

SYDNEY PARKINSON, the artist on Captain Cook's *Endeavour*, made the first drawing of an Australian parrot (a Red-tailed Black-Cockatoo) in 1770.

A LARGE FLOCK of cockatoos can totally defoliate a stand of trees in just hours and can also wreak havoc on wooden houses.

GLOSSY BLACK-COCKATOOS rely solely on she-oak seeds for their diet.

ONLY THE MALE Gang-Gang Cockatoo (*Callocephalon fimbriatum*, below) has a bright red head; females are a dull grey with red and yellow speckles on the chest.

COURTSHIP COCKATOO STYLE

Cockatoos mate for life and some routinely return to the same nesting hollow to lay eggs. Pairs strengthen their relationship with regular neck-rubbing and mutual preening. Most species breed in spring, after which females lay 1–6 eggs into a leaf-lined nest in a tree hollow. In white cockatoo species, both parents take responsibility for egg incubation. Only the female of black-cockatoo species is responsible for incubating and rearing chicks.

BACK IN BLACK

There are five species of black-cockatoo with the large Yellow-tailed Black-Cockatoo (*Calyptorhynchus funereus*) being the most common. The Short-billed Black-Cockatoo (or Carnaby's Cockatoo) is unique to South-West Western Australia. It is one of just two global white-tailed black cockatoo species.

Black-Cockatoos exhibit a remarkable behavioural trait not found in any other parrot or cockatoo species. For unknown reasons they always back into their nesting cavities. It may be that this is to protect them from snakes, as it would be more important for them to protect their heads than their tails if a snake were lying in wait.

Left: Female Red-tailed Black-Cockatoos are speckled and lack the round cheek patches of their more attractive male partners.

Parrots
— charismatic & colourful

Order: Psittaciformes
Family: Psittacidae

Parrots are known as Psittaciformes and have no close avian relatives, although they are distantly related to doves and pigeons. Australia has approximately 55 species of parrot and has often been called "the Land of Parrots" because of the abundance of species.

the FACTS!

SUPERB PARROTS fly in flocks that are separated by age, with adults in one flock and juveniles in another.

ROSELLAS (below) take their name from their first-sighted location — Rose Hill in Sydney, New South Wales. They were abundant at Rose Hill in the 1700s and become known as the Rose Hill Parrot, which was shortened to Rose Hillers and, later, Rosellas.

THE PARADISE PARROT (*Psephotus pulcherrimus*) was last sighted in 1927 and is believed to be extinct. Some specimens of this beautiful green, red, yellow and purple parrot were taken to England in the mid 1800s but, despite best efforts to get them to breed, soon died out.

AUSTRALIAN KING-PARROTS (*Alisterus scapularis*) nest very high in living trees that are hollowed out within the trunk. Despite the nest's high entrance, the hollow may penetrate almost to the ground.

The Superb Parrot (*Polytelis swainsonii*) has one of the most limited ranges, inhabiting just a small area of New South Wales. Habitat clearing and illegal trapping have reduced its numbers greatly.

TWO DISTINGUISHING FEATURES separate parrots from other bird families — zygodactylus feet and a short, sharp curving beak. The lower part of a parrot's jaw moves up and down; the upper part is hinged at the base, allowing some movement. Hence the upper part of the beak can hold a nut or seed steady while the lower part crushes it. Parrots are unable to chew, so once they crack open a nut they swallow the kernel whole. Gnawing on wood helps parrots keep their bills sharp. Although parrots are not songbirds, they are highly vocal screechers and squawkers and are excellent mimics. Most parrots are sociable and gregarious seed-eaters that fly in large flocks where many eyes make it easy to evade predators. Parrots' eyes can move independently of each other — a feature known as "monocular vision".

WANTED: HOLLOWS

Like nearly all parrots, Mulga Parrots (*Psephotus varius*, right) nest in tree hollows, which may take many years to form in eucalypt trees. Nests are lined with bark, leaves and feathers and keep eggs and chicks safe from terrestrial predators. Deforestation can affect parrot species. It is believed that only the lack of nesting hollows is limiting some species from increasing their distribution.

Conservation Watch

The Tasmanian Orange-bellied Parrot (left) is Australia's most endangered bird. Fewer than 400 of these spectacular birds exist in the wild. The Princess Parrot (far left) is also rare in the wild.

THE MOST COLOURFUL

Australia's parrots are some of the most brightly coloured birds in the world. As its species name suggests, one of the most splendidly attired is the male Scarlet-chested Parrot (*Neophema splendida*, top left). The Scarlet-chested Parrot was first described by John Gould in 1841. It inhabits mallee and Mulga scrubland throughout Victoria, South Australia, Western Australia and the southern Northern Territory. Despite its sky blue and cobalt head and wings, green back, bright red chest and yellow underbody, it cannot truly be said to be Australia's most colourful parrot species! Amazing as it may seem, the honour of being the most colourful has to go to the humble Budgerigar (bottom left). Although in the wild the Budgerigar is always green, it has the distinction of being the world's most colourful bird because breeding in captivity has introduced many thousands of possible budgie colour forms.

PAIRING UP

Most parrots pair for life. To sustain their romance, the males continue to court the females anew each year, as if for the first time. In species where one parent only incubates the eggs, they are usually fed entirely by the other partner until the chicks are old enough to be left.

Below left: Unlike many other parrot species, male and female lorikeets often look very similar and most species are vividly coloured. This pair are Rainbow Lorikeets (*Trichoglossus haematodus*), a common lorikeet species.

Below right: The blue and crimson female Eclectus Parrot looks very different from her green male counterpart. The two sexes look so different that they were thought to be different species when recorded in 1776.

the FACTS!

PARROTS, LIKE HUMANS, yawn often. When they do, their yawns are contagious and may set other parrots yawning as well.

THE RECLUSIVE Night Parrot (*Pezoporus occidentalis*) was believed extinct until Australian Museum ornithologist Walter Boles found one dead on the roadside near Boulia, Queensland, in 1990. However, further investigations have failed to verify the existence of these parrots, despite subsequent sightings. Their secretive lifestyle could be the reason they are so hard to find, presuming they still exist.

AUSTRALIA HAS SIX recognised rosella species and all of them have blue underwing coverts. They can be told apart from lorikeets because their tails are much broader. They are also characterised by bright cheek-patches, which are not seen in lorikeet species.

ALEX, an African Grey Parrot that was raised at the University of Minnesota, USA, learned the name of hundreds of objects. He could also count to six and say dozens of phrases. Sometimes he would even apologise if he bit someone!

DNA RESEARCH has shown that lorikeets have a slightly different genetic make-up to other parrots, so are grouped into the subfamily Loriinae. Australia has seven lorikeet species out of the world's 55 species. Lorikeets have a highly specialised brush-tipped tongue suited to their nectareous diet.

GRAEME CHAPMAN

Chick swindlers
— cuckoos, koels & coucals

Order: Cuculiformes
Families: Cuculidae & Centropodidae

Birds' natural instincts to protect and feed their young are exploited by one group of birds that can only be described as bad bird parents! Cuckoos lay their eggs in the nests of unsuspecting hosts — letting someone else do the hard work of raising and feeding their young.

the FACTS!

THE LITTLE BRONZE-CUCKOO (*Chrysococcyx minutillus*, above) is a rainforest species that lays its eggs mostly in the nest of gerygones.

A BABY CUCKOO hoists other fledglings or eggs out of the nest by balancing them on the flat middle of its back, between the wings, then struggling to the nest's side and heaving the chick over the edge.

BRONZE-CUCKOOS, such as Horsfield's Bronze-Cuckoo (*Chrysococcyx basalis*, below) have bars or bands on the feathers on their chests and a metallic sheen to the plumage on their backs.

A SINGLE GROWING CUCKOO needs a lot of food — more than a single chick of the host species. However, for some reason cuckoos convince their foster parents to bring the same amount of food that an entire nest full of their own chicks would need. Scientists thought the cuckoo's huge size made the foster parent bring more food, but research conducted in 2001 at Cambridge University in the UK showed that it was actually the cuckoo's call that kept the foster parent on the run. Studies found that the call of the Common Cuckoo, when analysed with a sonagraph, was nearly identical to calls made by an entire nest of warbler chicks.

RAOUL SLATER

A fledgling little bronze-cuckoo quickly ejects other eggs from the nest.

SUFFERING THE CONSEQUENCES

Trying to determine and kick out a potential cuckoo egg could have dire consequences for a bird's own chicks if the parent is mistaken. As a result, some species accept cuckoo eggs rather than risk destroying their own eggs. Visibility is a crucial factor in being able to spot a suspect egg. Species that have dark, cup-shaped nests frequently put up with intruders' eggs; however, species with more open nests that have better visibility can sometimes determine a cuckoo egg and toss it out of the nest.

If only birds knew what to look for they could easily distinguish cuckoo nestlings from their own chicks once they hatched. Unlike baby passerines, hatchling cuckoos have zygodactylous feet, rounded nostrils and a distinct lack of down feathers. Amazingly, most host species (with the exception of the Superb Fairy-wren) are unable to tell that something is horribly wrong with their chick — even when the chick is twice as big and looks nothing like its parents!

M & I MORCOMBE

KILLER BABIES

Cuckoo eggs may cunningly match the shading of their host species or may look nothing like them, but many birds do not notice the difference and incubate these little parasites-in-waiting. Within 48 hours of hatching, cuckoo chicks go on a murderous mission — pushing other unhatched eggs or chicks out of the nest so they can have their "adopted" parent all to themselves.

GRAEME CHAPMAN

Honeyeaters with larger-than-life chicks continue to play surrogate mum to cuckoos.

Conservation Watch

The Chestnut-breasted Cuckoo (*Cacomantis castaneiventris*) is a rarely seen migrant to tropical rainforest near the tip of Cape York, Queensland.

PLUS-SIZED PARASITES

At up to 65 cm, the Channel-billed Cuckoo (*Scythrops novaehollandiae*) is the largest parasitic bird in the world. It visits Australia during summer to breed and is sometimes called the "Rainbird" or "Stormbird" because in Australia's north it seems to herald the wet season. Channel-billed Cuckoos lay their deceptive eggs in the nests of the Torresian Crow, Australian Raven, Australian Magpie, Pied Currawong and Collared Sparrowhawk.

Above, left to right: Channel-billed Cuckoos are large — about the size of a small raptor species. Surprisingly, their foster parents often continue to feed them even when the chick is larger than them! This Pied Currawong is surely wondering why its chick is so big and so hungry.

KOELS ARE CUCKOOS

Common Koels (*Eudynamys scolopacea*) are a type of cuckoo that migrate to Australia from New Guinea and South-East Asia in spring and early summer and lay their own eggs in the nests of other birds. Although they are absent mothers when the chicks are hatched, mother koels are reunited with their offspring once the young koels fledge. By the end of summer, they leave with their young to migrate back to their place of origin.

COUCAL NOT CUCKOO

The Pheasant Coucal (*Centropus phasianinus*) is the sole member of the family Centropodidae. They are more closely related to cuckoos than they are to pheasants — a name they acquired because of their long pheasant-like tail. Pheasant Coucals differ from cuckoos in that they are mostly ground-dwelling birds that raise their own young, rather than being parasitic. Both parents construct a nest in a flattened grass tussock or in a low tree and both incubate and feed their offspring.

the FACTS!

THE PALLID CUCKOO (*Cuculus pallidus*) is the most widespread species of cuckoo in Australia. It lays its eggs into the nests of an estimated 80 host species.

UNUSUALLY for cuckoos, the Channel-billed Cuckoo is largely a fruit-eater that feasts on figs and other native fruits.

BECAUSE of the Channel-billed Cuckoo's size, it often damages the host's eggs when attempting to lay its own eggs in the nest. However, unlike other cuckoos, baby Channel-billed Cuckoos do not throw their "siblings" out of the nest when they hatch. They prefer to starve them by stealing all of the food the host parent brings to the nest.

FAN-TAILED CUCKOOS (*Cacomantis flabelliformis*, below) are characterised by the yellow ring around the eyes.

KOELS are migrants that have a truly Aussie call — males make a ringing, two note "coo-ee" vocalisation.

YOUNG KOELS have brown eyes while adults have red eyes.

PHEASANT COUCALS make a distinctive "oop-oop-oop" call.

Night hunters
— owls, frogmouths & relatives

Orders: Strigiformes & Caprimulgiformes
Families: Tytonidae, Strigidae, Caprimulgidae, Aegothelidae & Podargidae

Long associated with wisdom, wide-eyed owls are the silent night hunters of the bird world. Incredible eyesight, hearing and soft, feathery wings help them to stealthily swoop down on prey in the darkness.

the FACTS!

IN THE DREAMING STORIES of the Worora Aboriginal people of Western Australia, the first owl was called Dunbi. When a group of children teased and tormented Dunbi, he caused a fierce storm that swept away and killed all of the inhabitants of Earth, leaving only one man and one woman.

BARKING OWLS (*Ninox connivens*) make a deep rumbling growl followed by a series of "woof woofs" when they feel threatened.

IN THE BLUE MOUNTAINS, NSW, one frequently used roosting site for the Sooty Owl (*Tyto tenebricosa*, below) has a huge accumulation of pellets, some of which can be dated back 17,000 years! Some of the bones and body parts found in this mass of pellets belong to animals that no longer exist in the area.

OWLS IN THE GENUS *NINOX* have smaller heads and larger eyes, and are often called hawk-owls. They lay 2–4 eggs once a year, compared to the more irregular breeding of birds in the genus *Tyto*, which lay 2–6 eggs in each clutch, sometimes twice a year.

SUPER SENSES

Owls have the best night vision on the planet! Although they may appear round, owls eyes are actually elongated. They do not move in the eye sockets, so if an owl wants to look to one side it must turn its head. To enable it to do this effectively, an owl has fourteen vertebrae in its neck — twice as many as a human! Consequently, its head can twist 270° (three-quarters of a circle). Owls have binocular vision (each eye's area of vision overlaps to take in a field of view of about 110°), which is required for judging distance and speed when hunting prey.

As well as exceptional eyesight, owls have excellent hearing. They can hear noises that are ten times fainter than those heard by the human ear. A peculiar quirk makes owls able to identify where a sound is coming from with pinpoint accuracy — one of their ear openings is higher than the other. This asymmetry means that owls do not have to turn their heads to determine the location of a sound. An owl's medulla — the part of the brain that governs hearing — is far more complex than that of other birds. *Tyto* genus owls are even better hearers because the disc-shape of their faces works a bit like a satellite disc, funnelling sound towards the owl's ears.

Owls make little noise. Such silence has a twofold advantage — it does not obscure other noises and its stops prey from hearing the owl's approach. For this reason, night-hunting owls have unique wing features to streamline their flight to a relatively silent swoop. Soft, fluffy body feathers absorb and "pillow" the sound, keeping the owl's approach stealthy.

The Southern Boobook is the smallest and most commonly seen owl species in Australia. It is sometimes also called the Mopoke, after its soft "mo-poke" call.

Conservation Watch

Christmas Island is the only place where the Christmas Island Hawk-Owl (*Ninox natalis*) survives. About 1000 remain in the wild. The Lesser Sooty Owl (*Tyto multipunctata*) is restricted to a small area of mountain rainforest in north Queensland.

BIRD OR BRANCH?

Tawny Frogmouths (*Podargus strigoides*) are masters of camouflage that are related to owls and nightjars. Unlike owls (which have forward-facing eyes), frogmouths and nightjars have eyes that are situated on either side of the head. Their feet are also different from an owl's feet. Owls have feathered legs with talons for seizing prey. In contrast, Tawny Frogmouths have small, soft feet that they use only for perching. Tawny Frogmouths hunt in a similar fashion to kookaburras, sitting very still and camouflaging themselves on branches until prey comes close. They are the only Australian bird species that can eat poisonous Christmas Beetles. Tawny Frogmouths mate for life and take turns raising the young, sitting on the eggs in shifts (the male takes the day shift and swaps with the female at night). Parents chase chicks away three months after they have fledged.

A Tawny Frogmouth will point its head skywards and sit perfectly still to resemble a tree branch.

HIDE & SEEK

Relatives of the frogmouths that share the order Caprimulgiformes are nightjars. The Australian Owlet-nightjar (*Aegotheles cristatus*) is the only local species of the family Aegothelidae. Mainland Australia has three species of nightjar, the White-throated (*Eurostopodus mystacalis*), Spotted (*E. argus*) and Large-tailed (*Caprimulgus macrurus*). Streaky, speckled brown, buff and grey colouration allows nightjars to conceal themselves perfectly on logs and branches, either on the ground, in the tree tops or among dead leaves. In fact, they are so well camouflaged that bushwalkers sometimes step on these masters of disguise as they conceal themselves by day. The Owlet-nightjar has a slightly different, but still effective, method of concealment. It hides by day in tree hollows, where its large eyes and mottled grey-brown feathers mean it is often mistaken for a Sugar Glider peering out from a tree hollow.

The Spotted Nightjar is the most colourful nightjar species, enabling it to blend in with stony, clay or ochre sands and soils.

Australian Owlet-nightjars are widespread and live in numerous habitats throughout Australia, where they hide by day and hunt at night.

the FACTS!

MALE TAWNY FROGMOUTHS are incredibly territorial and often attack an intruding frogmouth's mouth, sometimes even tearing out their tongue. Luckily for Tawny Frogmouths, they can regrow their tongue if this happens!

OWLS tear apart their prey and swallow it bones, feathers, fur and all. Indigestible parts, such as bones, beaks and claws, are later regurgitated in pellet form.

THE SOUTHERN BOOBOOK (*Ninox novaeseelandiae*), endemic to Lord Howe Island, became locally extinct there in the 1950s when the Tasmanian Masked Owl (*Tyto novaehollandieae castanops*) was introduced to control rats. The Tasmanian Masked Owl is also affecting populations of the Lord Howe Island Woodhen and White Tern. At around 57 cm, the Tasmanian Masked Owl is the largest *Tyto* owl on Earth.

THE BARN OWL (*Tyto alba*, below) exists on every continent except Antarctica. Barn owls eat an average of three animals a day.

ONLY ONE SPECIES of Australian owl nests on the ground, the Grass Owl (*Tyto capensis*). It is also the only owl to hunt on the wing (sometimes even hunting by day). It is easily distinguished from other species because it has exceptionally long legs — up to 15% longer than those of Australia's other owl species.

Kookaburras,
kingfishers & relatives

Order: Coraciiformes
Family: Alcedinidae, Halcyonidae, Meropidae & Coraciidae

The Laughing Kookaburra is perhaps the bird that Australians best relate to — because with its laughter-like call it seems to have an excellent sense of humour. What many people do not know is that kookaburras are actually the largest members of the kingfisher family.

the FACTS!

THE FOREST KINGFISHER (*Todiramphus macleayii*, above) has a race, *macleayii*, that is found only in the Northern Territory. Another race, *incinctus*, is found from Cape York down the eastern coast to South Australia.

THE BUFF-BREASTED Paradise-Kingfisher migrates annually from New Guinea to Australia, which is an arduous, energy-consuming voyage. Why it chooses to do this when other paradise-kingfisher species do not, is the question. It may be that competition for nest sites in termite mounds is stiff in New Guinea, whereas birds can find plenty of termite mounds on Australia's Cape York Peninsula.

KINGFISHERS and kookaburras have weakly perching toes and are unable to walk; instead, they have to hop when on the ground.

BEE-EATERS (below) court by vibrating their tails and raising the feathers on the tops of their heads. Males also offer the females food to entice them to mate. To nest, they excavate burrows in riverbanks or paddocks that have soft soil. The female does most of the nest building and digs a tunnel that is up to a metre long with a chamber at the end. Both parents rear the young.

KINGFISHERS are small, swift birds that snatch up insects from the air or from the ground, or dive into water after yabbies and fish. Two larger species are commonly known as kookaburras, the Blue-winged (*Dacelo leachii*) and Laughing (*D. novaeguineae*) Kookaburra.

M & I MORCOMBE

A Sacred Kingfisher (*Todiramphus sanctus*) returns to its nest hollow with a tasty treat.

Perching on a branch above the water is the Azure Kingfisher's usual hunting strategy.

Rather than actively hunting, kookaburras and kingfishers rely on a perch-and-pounce technique — patiently waiting for their prey to come close to them. When a prey animal comes by, they pounce. Two kingfisher species, the Azure (*Alcedo azurea*) and Little (*A. pusilla*) Kingfishers, prefer to live and hunt near rivers and other waterways.

Eight other species, including the Laughing Kookaburra, Sacred Kingfisher, Yellow-billed Kingfisher (*Syma torotoro*) and Red-backed Kingfisher (*Todiramphus pyrrhopygia*) are birds of the forests and woodlands that prey largely on invertebrates such as centipedes and grubs, although the Sacred Kingfisher and Collared Kingfisher also scoop up fish and aquatic animals. Forest-dwelling species usually have wider, flatter bills than their river-living relatives.

The small, vividly blue Forest Kingfisher waiting for any sign of insects or other invertebrate prey in its forest habitat.

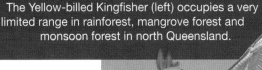

Conservation Watch

The Yellow-billed Kingfisher (left) occupies a very limited range in rainforest, mangrove forest and monsoon forest in north Queensland.

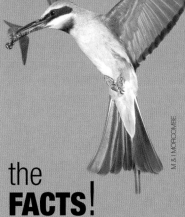

the
FACTS!

THE RAINBOW BEE-EATER
(above) is Australia's only bee-eater species. Bee-eaters catch their meals on the wing and can eat as many as 100 bees each day.

IF A PAIR OF KOOKABURRAS
has been unable to raise their own young, they sometimes "adopt" from another group or clan if they require extra members.

BABY KOOKABURRAS do not
defecate in the nest. Instead, they turn around and hang their tails off the side of the nest and squirt their runny faeces outside.

YOUNG KOOKABURRAS are
unable to make the laughing call that adults make; instead, they practise making wheezy, rasping sounds until they master the call.

RAISING THE TAIL very high is
a signal to others to stay away in kookaburra body language.

ONLY ONE REPRESENTATIVE
of the bird family known as rollers is a regular visitor to Australia. The Dollarbird (*Eurystomus orientalis*, below), so named for the round dollar-sized patches under its wings, breeds annually in Australia.

FAITHFUL PARTNERS

It may take a Laughing Kookaburra (above left) as long as 5–7 years to find a partner, but like Blue-winged Kookaburras (above right) they mate for life. Kookaburras need around 5 ha for their breeding territory. Although kookaburras pair for life, males court their partners with tidbits and remodel their nest sites every year. To impress his partner, the male uses loud laughter, tail flicking and wing fluttering before bringing her a gift of food, such as a grub or lizard. When the female attempts to grab the food, the male refuses to release it until the female kookaburra makes a special sound that lets him know she consents to be his partner. Males build the nest by finding a soft spot or knot on a gum tree and hollowing it out until it is large enough to accommodate five kookaburras. The female inspects his handiwork, but may still reject it out of hand and fly off to find another site. If she does this, the poor male is forced to begin again.

The nest is a kookaburra killing field, particularly for the smallest chick. Blue-winged Kookaburras may also be found to kill their siblings, as they have a similar hooked beak when young.

NEST NASTINESS

The kookaburra's laughter may make it sound cheerful, but nest life for Laughing Kookaburra siblings is anything but fun! Young kookaburras routinely starve or kill a sibling — an action that adult kookaburras seem to ignore. Unlike most birds' clutches, Laughing Kookaburra's eggs hatch at different times, leaving the youngest and smallest chick very vulnerable. Usually, the third egg is simply insurance in case the other chicks fall prey to predators, so the parent turns a blind eye to nest violence. Even nature seems to favour this form of "siblicide" — baby kookaburras are born with temporary hooked beaks that seem purpose-built for attacking siblings! Strangely, however, while nest mates are murderous, older siblings from a previous clutch are helpful. Adolescent kookaburras often help feed newly hatched chicks — a trait seen in just 3% of bird species.

Mound-building
megapodes

Order: Galliformes
Family: Megapodiidae

Australia is home to three species of mound-building bird belonging to the family Megapodiidae — the Australian Brush-turkey, the Orange-footed Scrubfowl and the Malleefowl. All have large feet for scraping together soil and leaf litter to construct elaborate mounds.

the FACTS!

IN 2004, research conducted by Macquarie University and the University of Queensland determined something that Indigenous Australians had been aware of for some time — that temperature affects the sex of brush-turkey chicks. If the temperature of the mound is consistently kept at 34°C, equal numbers of male and female chicks hatch. However, when the temperature falls to 31°C, more males hatch and at 36°C or more, only females hatch. The sex of the embryos in the eggs was not determined by temperature, but it did affect which eggs would hatch.

BECAUSE Australian Brush-turkey chicks have no contact with their parents or siblings, researchers often wondered how they recognised others of their kind to breed later in life. Now, robots are helping them figure this out! Scientists from Macquarie University used robots covered in the skins of dead chicks to study whether the chicks recognised their own. The robots mimicked common brush-turkey actions such as pecking and scanning (moving the head from side to side). One even had UV filters to block out any UV markings (which cannot be seen by the human eye) that might have played a part. Scientists found that a combination of pecking and UV light might help these birds recognise a potential mate.

THE MALAU, the world's smallest and rarest megapode species, lives in Polynesia and lays its eggs near volcanic vents, where it uses the hot ash and soil to incubate its eggs!

OF AUSTRALIA'S three megapodes, the most commonly seen is the red-headed Australian Brush-turkey (*Alectura lathami*). Like all other megapode males, one of the most important tasks of the male Australian Brush-turkey's existence is the creation of the mound nest.

A metre-high mound is constructed of leaf litter and decomposing organic material, which, as it decomposes, keeps the eggs warm. It must be kept at a consistent temperature of 32–34°C to ensure as many chicks as possible hatch. If the nest becomes too hot, it is the male's task to scratch away some of the mound covering. If the nest gets too cold, he

Brush-turkeys can fly if necessary and will roost in low branches at night, although they are mostly ground-dwelling.

uses his feet to pile on some hot sand or more warming cover. To check the temperature, the brush-turkey uses a built-in thermometer — its beak and head! The bare skin on the brush-turkey's head, plus sensitive receptors on his beak, help him figure out whether the nest is too hot, too cold or just right. Strangely, after all this nest maintenance, he does not even hang around to ensure his chicks hatch safely. When the eggs hatch, the chicks are on their own and must dig their way out of the nest and set off in search of food.

The small, 40 cm long Orange-footed Scrubfowl (*Megapodius reinwardt*) also builds a mound and has no contact with its young. Sometimes several pairs of scrubfowl share the same mound nest.

FOWL OF THE MALLEE

Malleefowl (*Leipoa ocellata*) are slightly smaller than the Australian Brush-turkey and roam the dry scrub of the southern Australian mainland. They are the only megapodes that are able to live in arid regions because much of their liquid nourishment comes from their diet of fruit, seeds, herbs and juicy insects, which allows them to survive quite well without water. A speckled pattern of white, black and red-brown helps camouflage them among the sticks and gravel of their dappled scrubland habitat.

Right: Seen from the front, the Malleefowl has a brown stripe running from its beak to its breast). It also has a small crest. Malleefowls are mostly terrestrial, but if threatened they will fly short distances.

MOUNDS WITH THERMOSTATS

Like the male Australian Brush-turkey and Orange-footed Scrubfowl, the Malleefowl is also a dedicated mound builder. Approximately 9–11 months of a male Malleefowl's year are taken up with the task of constructing and maintaining his "incubator". After mating, females lay one large egg in the nest every 3–7 days, upon which the male must again check the nest temperature. In each breeding season the female Australian Brush-turkey may lay as many as 35 eggs!

Decaying matter in the huge 2–5 m high and 12 m wide nest incubates the eggs for 60–90 days, after which time the originally pale pink eggs will have turned a dark beige in colour. During the entire incubation period, it is the male's job to make sure that the temperature within the mound remains at 32–34°C. When the chicks hatch, they must struggle their way up through the dense covering of vegetation to the outside world. Just an hour after they leave the nest they can run, and within a day they fly off for a solitary life until it is time for them to begin to breed.

the FACTS!

MALE AND FEMALE
Malleefowls mate for life.

NEST MOUNDS (below) can be more than a metre deep and it can take some chicks 2–15 hours to dig their way out of the mound.

SOME MALLEEFOWL MOUNDS can be as much as 12 m wide!

MANY MALLEEFOWL CHICKS do not survive the first few weeks of life and die of starvation or predation. Researchers estimate that only around 2% Malleefowl hatchlings survive to adulthood.

CHICKS THAT DO SURVIVE may go on to enjoy a relatively long life. Malleefowls can live for 25–35 years in the wild.

PROGURA NARACOORTENSIS was a giant megafauna Malleefowl that became extinct about 35,000 years ago. Its fossilised remains were found in Naracoorte Cave in South Australia.

Using their strong back legs, male Malleefowls excavate a deep pit into which the female lays eggs. They then maintain the mound's temperature until the chicks hatch around three months later.

Ground-lovers
— true quails & "false" quails

Order: Galliformes & Turniciformes
Families: Phasianidae & Turnicidae

The Painted Button-quail (*Turnix varia*) is one of seven local button-quail species. Physical and behavioural differences place button-quails in a different family from true quails.

the FACTS!

THREE INTRODUCED SPECIES of game bird are also found in Australia — the Common Pheasant (*Phasianus colchicus*), the Indian Peafowl (*Pavo cristatus*) and the Red Junglefowl (*Gallus gallus*).

BANDING RECORDS have shown that the Stubble Quail can make long flights — sometimes covering distances of up to 1100 km.

MALE KING QUAILS (*Coturnix chinensis*, below) are more colourful than females, with a white bib, grey body and rufous underbelly. The colour difference indicates that in this species it is the female that incubates the egg and therefore needs more subtle camouflage colours.

FEMALE BUTTON-QUAILS may mate with as many as seven males in each mating season.

BUTTON-QUAILS ARE SHY and secretive. If alarmed, they freeze or burst from underfoot in a short, whirring flight. When cautious, they exhibit a strange, tentative gait whereby they creep forwards while rocking back and forwards.

Stumpy, short-winged quails, of which there are three native species, are Galliformes that are not in any way related to the Turniciformes — a family which includes the quails' namesakes, button-quails.

ALL TRUE AND "FALSE" QUAILS

have small wings and eat and nest on the ground. Differences are both anatomical and behavioural. Button-quails have only three toes, which all point forwards, while true quails all have four toes, three that point forwards and one backwards. Breeding behaviour also differs in that button-quails practise polyandry, so males incubate eggs and raise young.

IAN MCCANN/ANT PHOTO

TRUE QUAILS

Native quails are omnivorous and feed on insects as well as the shoots, seeds and herbaceous leaves of plants and crops, particularly those growing near rivers and streams. Nests are simple scrapes on the ground or under grass tussocks and bushes and are usually lined with grass. Females lay 4–11 eggs, which they incubate themselves (although males help out once the eggs hatch and both parents feed the hatchlings).

BUTTON-QUAILS

There are seven local button-quail species, including the Red-chested (*Turnix pyrrhothorax*), Red-backed (*T. maculosa*) and Little Button-quail (*T. velox*). Female button-quails are solitary, territorial and dominant when it comes to breeding. Using a loud booming call, they attract the male and often gift him with food before mating and laying eggs, which he then incubates for two weeks before raising the hatchlings alone.

A male Little Button-quail brooding. The specked colouring helps him blend in.

M & I MORCOMBE

Earth & arbor
— pittas & treecreepers

Conservation Watch
One pitta species, the Red-bellied Pitta (*Pitta erythrogaster*), is a rare breeding migrant to Australia from New Guinea.

Order: Passeriformes
Families: Climacteridae & Pittadae

Although they can fly well, tiny bright pittas prefer to dwell on the forest floor, where they forage in leaf litter. In some areas of their range, they share their habitat with the unrelated treecreepers — skilled, gravity-defying tree-climbers that probe and peck at bark for an insect meal.

CLAWED TREE-CLIMBERS

Six treecreeper species inhabit a range of Australian habitats. The most common is the Brown Treecreeper (*Climacteris picumnus*), which prefers woodlands from eastern South Australia to Cape York in Queensland. Treecreepers have modified perching feet with strong claws that help them hop up tree trunks, clinging to the surface and sometimes even dangling upside down to peck at invertebrates.

The Rufous Treecreeper (*Climacteris rufa*) is the most colourful treecreeper species.

THE PITTA PATTER
OF LITTLE FEET

Shy little pittas come from a large and ancient family, with an estimated 23–31 living species worldwide. Members of the family are found from South-East Asia to India and Africa, with three native Australian species. Female pittas lay up to four eggs into a dome-shaped nest of twigs and vegetation lined with dung, grass or decaying wood, and both pitta parents take turns brooding and feeding the young once they hatch.

Brightly plumed pittas are sometimes also known as "jewel-thrushes". The Noisy Pitta (*Pitta versicolor*) is one of the most commonly seen pittas and is found along the east coast from northern New South Wales to the tip of Cape York.

the FACTS!

APART FROM THE COMMON White-throated Treecreeper, all treecreepers employ the help of offspring from previous clutches to help them raise new nestlings.

TREECREEPERS SOMETIMES follow a trail of ants up a tree trunk, gobbling up an ant with each upwards hop. Once it reaches the canopy, the treecreeper spirals down to the ground and starts again.

UNLIKE AMERICAN WOODPECKERS, treecreepers (like the Brown Treecreeper, below) use tree hollows rather than drill or peck out their own nest.

PITTA IS AN INDIAN WORD from the area around Madras. It simply means "bird" and came to be used exclusively for these types of birds in the 1700s.

CLEVER PITTAS use "anvils" to help them get into hard snail shells. They place the snail on a rock or piece of wood and batter it with their stout beaks until the shell cracks and they can get at the juicy flesh inside. Some birds use the same anvil over and over until the stone becomes worn and polished by this avian shell-smith.

THE NOISY PITTA'S call sounds like "walk to work, walk to work"!

Bright bush gems
— wrens, robins & pardalotes

Order: Passeriformes
Families: Maluridae, Petroicidae & Pardalotidae

Australia's wren and robin species are not really wrens or robins at all! English settlers named them after similar species found in Europe, but the similarities are entirely superficial.

ASIDE FROM A FEW NEW GUINEAN SPECIES, fairy-wrens exist only in Australia, where they are a common sight flitting around parks and gardens, with their long tails held erect. Less well known are the similar but secretive grasswren and emu-wren species, which occupy more isolated areas than the fairy-wrens. All of them live in small groups and are assumed to nest cooperatively, with dominant males advertising their territory by singing from high vantage points.

the FACTS!

THE GENUS NAME of the Eastern Yellow Robin (*Eopsaltria australis*, above) means "dawn harpist" because they sing to usher in the dawn.

FEMALE SUPERB FAIRY-WRENS defend a small territory with the help of up to three of their male offspring and their partners.

FAIRY-WRENS mimic rodents to lure predators away from nests and vulnerable chicks. Dropping flat on the ground, with wings to the side and the tail lowered, they scuttle off like a mouse.

THE BEAUTIFUL Red-capped Robin (*Petroica goodenovii*, below) is the smallest and most brightly coloured robin.

MARTIN WILLIS

THE RUFOUS-CROWNED Emu-wren (*Stipiturus ruficeps*) remained undiscovered for more than 100 years after European settlement of Australia. It occupies spinifex country in the arid interior.

THE BLACK GRASSWREN (*Amytornis housei*) lives in such inaccessible and remote regions in the Kimberley that scientists have not yet been able to discover much about its nesting habits.

Superb Fairy-wrens (*Malurus cyaneus*) grow to a maximum size of about 14 cm. They are common around grasslands, shrubland and heath along the continent's east coast.

SUPERB DETECTIVES

The Superb Fairy-wren has a unique ability — it is the only bird able to identify cuckoo chicks in its nest and evict the parasitic babies. Studies conducted at the Australian National University found that although the fairy-wrens could not distinguish their own eggs from the eggs of Horsfield's Bronze-cuckoo, partly due to their dark nests, once the eggs hatched they were able to tell that the baby cuckoo was not one of their own. Newly hatched cuckoos usually toss out all other eggs and hatchlings within 48 hours of hatching. However, one of the triggers for the fairy-wrens seems to be a single chick in the nest. Researchers found that in 40% of cases, Superb Fairy-wrens left solo impostors to starve but were far less likely to desert the nest if the single chick was of their own species. The cuckoo chick's call may have helped alert the fairy-wrens.

ROBINS

Australian robins, of which there are about 21 species, actually evolved tens of millions of years ago and are not related to the robins of Europe. Most of them are birds of the grass or shrubby understorey of forest and woodlands, where they search for insects and other invertebrates. All of them create cup-shaped nests and incubate 2–4 eggs for a little over two weeks. Males and females of most species are similar in colour, with the males sometimes having plumage that is slightly brighter than the females'.

Right: An Eastern Yellow Robin on the nest

DAINTY FAIRY-WRENS

Fairy-wrens mostly live in small groups in which a breeding pair is assisted by last season's offspring. Although most birds are intolerant of other sexually mature adults in their breeding territory, fairy-wrens seem unconcerned. They have a complex social structure and are cooperative breeders, which means that other birds remain in the territory to help the dominant male and female to protect and feed their young. Only the dominant male in each group is adorned in full breeding plumage. Male "attendants" will not breed in the group unless the dominant male dies, but sometimes they exhibit full breeding colours. When environmental conditions are good, fairy-wrens increase the number of eggs in their clutch. In spite of their many "helpers" it is estimated that almost half of the fairy-wren eggs laid and chicks born do not live to fledge.

Beautiful cobalt blue White-winged Fairy-wrens also have a black and white race on Dirk Hartog Island, WA.

The male Purple-crowned Fairy-wren (*Malurus coronatus*) has a prominent lilac crown that readily sets him apart from his plainer female companion.

The Red-backed Fairy-wren's (*Malurus melanocephalus*) scientific name means "black-headed", rather than "red-backed".

GRASSWRENS

Thanks to the isolated environments they inhabit, reclusive and endemic grasswrens are among the hardest to find of all Australian birds. Rocky country and arid shrublands in Central Australia, Western Australia and South Australia are their preferred habitats, so they rarely come into contact with anyone but the most enthusiastic birdwatcher. There are currently ten recognised species, with the Striated Grasswren (*Amytornis striatus*, below) being the most widespread.

PARDALOTES

Australia has four pardalote species and all forage among gum leaves for lerps (the sugary covering constructed by psyllid bugs) and suck at tree sap (manna). Pardalotes nest by digging a deep, long burrow in a creekbed or built-up road verge. Because it is so dark down in the burrow, pardalote chicks have a glow-in-the-dark gape. Special glowing patches at the side of the mouth help parents guide food into their chicks' mouths. Flinders, Maria and Bruny Islands, as well as dry sclerophyll forest of south-eastern Tasmania are the last refuges of the rare Forty-spotted Pardalote (*Pardalotus quadragintus*).

Left, top to bottom: Spotted Pardalote (*Pardalotus punctatus*); Striated Pardalote (*Pardalotus striatus*).

Nectar lovers
— honeyeaters & relatives

Order: Passeriformes
Families: Meliphagidae

M. & I MORCOMBE

the FACTS!

YELLOW-THROATED MINERS (*Manorina flavigula*, above) have yellowish feathers on the neck that set them apart from Noisy Miners.

NECTARIVOROUS honeyeaters have more pointed slender bills than species that are omnivorous and also eat more insects.

THE BLUE-FACED HONEYEATER (*Entomyzon cyanotis*, below) is a regular visitor to gardens in New South Wales and Queensland. Adults have a blue patch, or lores, around the eye, while a juvenile's eye patch is greenish yellow.

NOISY MINERS (*Manorina melanocephala*) are highly territorial birds that chase other birds from their feeding grounds and alert other members of their colony to danger with loud, piping calls. They regularly shriek, scream at and dive-bomb intruders such as cats, goannas and larger birds (such as kookaburras and crows).

FOUR LOCAL HONEYEATER species are known as friarbirds because their bald heads fringed with tufted grey feathers resemble the haircut of a friar. Three are also characterised by a large lump on the top of the beak.

M. & I MORCOMBE

A female Western Spinebill (*Acanthorhynchus superciliosus*) uses her long, curved bill to delicately extract nectar from a grevillea. The long, curved beaks of spinebills enable them to reach deep down into floral species that have sock-like flowers, such as Mountain Devils or heath.

Australia's honeyeater species, of which there are approximately 67, all have specially adapted brush-like tongues that probe the depths of nectar-filled plants, seeking the sugary substance. However, they do not subsist entirely on nectar. While nectar is high in carbohydrates, it contains no protein, which is required for growing feathers.

TO RECEIVE ENOUGH PROTEIN, most honeyeaters also eat insects and some rainforest species occasionally dine on fruit. However, for the most part they are superbly adapted to take advantage of some of the plants that have evolved side-by-side with them from Gondwanan times — plants in the families Proteaceae and Myrtaceae. A honeyeater's tongue is divided into four sections, each covered with tiny spongy hairs that soak up the sweet, sticky sap of honey-producing plants.

IN PURSUIT OF NECTAR

Most honeyeaters are nomadic, travelling in small flocks to make the most of the flowering seasons of certain floral species. Some, such as the Yellow-faced Honeyeater (*Lichenostomus chrysops*), even make long migrations from the north to the south of the continent in search of their sticky food source.

Right: After breeding season, Scarlet Honeyeaters wander nomadically in search of flowering plants.

PETER SLATER

Conservation Watch

The Black-eared Miner has a limited range in mallee scrub near the Murray River on the adjoining borders of NSW, SA and Vic.

POLLINATORS OF THE BUSH

Plant species enjoy a mutually beneficial relationship with honey-eating birds. In feasting on nectar, the bird's beak, feathers and feet frequently become laden with floury pollen. When the bird moves from one shrub or tree to the next, it carries with it the pollen from its previous stopover, which is transferred to the new flower. The birds are quickly and effectively depositing the pollinating substance directly into the plant's reproductive organs in the same way that pollen-eating insects would. Curiously, while Australia has evolved many pollinating bird species, not one of Europe's plant species is wholly reliant on birds to reproduce. Some birds have even developed special relationships with certain plant species. The rare Regent Honeyeater (*Xanthomyza phrygia*) has become a specialised feeder on the fruit and nectar of the parasitic mistletoe plant. Nectarivorous birds can also help trees remain healthy by eating the sweet larvae sacs (or lerps) of psyllid bugs that damage trees.

The continent's three wattlebird species are so named because of the dangling fleshy skin, or wattles, that hang from their cheeks.

HOVERING LIKE HUMMINGBIRDS

Unlike most other Australian bird species, some honeyeaters and spinebills are able to "hover", in a similar fashion to the hummingbird, by flapping their wings at such a rate that they can feed while still in the air — although they cannot sustain themselves in this activity for long. Australia has two spinebill species, the Eastern and Western Spinebill. Sunbirds (of the family Nectariniidae) can also beat their wings rapidly to hover in one spot while they suck up nectar through their slender, straw-like beaks.

Below, left to right: A Banded Honeyeater (*Certhionix pectoralis*) hovers in suspended animation below a food source; The hovering ability is also useful for feeding nestlings and entering the nest.

the FACTS!

MANY SPECIES of honeyeater bolster up their woven cup-shaped nests with cobwebs, lichen and even hair plucked from horses, cattle and dogs.

TASMANIA'S Yellow Wattlebird (*Anthochaera paradoxa*) is the world's largest nectarivore.

HONEYEATERS lap away at sticky plant stamens incredibly quickly — they can perform up to ten licks in just one second!

HONEYDEW is another favourite food for nectarivorous birds. It is made up of sugary secretions from plant-sucking insects.

DURING COURTSHIP, the Tawny-crowned Honeyeater (*Phylidonyris melanops*, below) flies high above the heathlands, then spirals downwards while singing a loud, lilting, melodious song.

BOTH THE RED and the Yellow Wattlebird were hunted extensively as gamebirds until they became fully protected in the early 1970s.

LEWIN'S HONEYEATER'S repetitive staccato call sounds somewhat like a machine-gun.

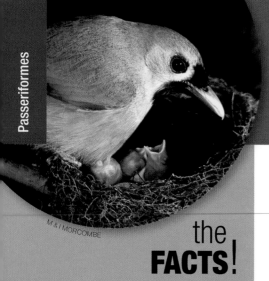

M & I MORCOMBE

Quite a tail
— flycatchers & relatives

Order: Passeriformes
Families: Dicruridae & Campephagidae

Fantails, monarchs, the Spangled Drongo, the common Willie Wagtail and the Magpie-lark belong to the Dicruridae family of small insectarivores that are famous for their expressive, splayed tails. Cuckoo-shrikes, in the family Campephagidae, are also renowned for a characteristic comfort movement. When they perch, the way they settle their wings has earned them the name "shufflewings".

the FACTS!

MONARCHS, such as the Black-faced Monarch (*Monarcha melanopsis*, above) are enthusiastic carollers during the breeding season. They go to great measures to protect their young, even attacking birds as large as hawks that venture into the monarch's territory.

MANY FLYCATCHING SPECIES have small bristly vibrissae around the mouth that help them guide insects into their mouths.

THE SPANGLED DRONGO (*Dicrurus bracteatus*, below) is resident in the country's north. Individual southern birds are either resident or migrate northwards in winter.

IAN MORRIS

UNUSUALLY FOR BIRDS, the female Shining Flycatcher (*Myiagra alecto*) is more colourful than her male partner, which is usually jet black.

THE WILLIE WAGTAIL'S chirruping song sounds like it is saying "sweet pretty creature".

FANTAILS & FLYCATCHERS

Four small insect-eating species in Australia are known as fantails and a further five are commonly called flycatchers. Along with tails that can be dramatically raised, lowered and spread out in a fan-like display, many of the flycatchers have small crests that can be raised slightly during breeding displays.

Fantails are fabulous nest architects. Grasses and cobwebs are tightly woven together to make a secure cup-shaped nest that is situated about 10 m above the ground on a tree branch and features a "tail" to drain off water. Flycatchers' nests do not "trail" but instead are made of strips of bark and thin tree roots securely fastened with cobwebs to a horizontal or vertical tree fork. To camouflage the nest, it is decorated around the rim with torn off bits of paperbark and, sometimes, lichen.

The Rufous Fantail (*Rhipidura rufifrons*) builds its nest, which terminates in a long dangling "tail", in wet sclerophyll forests.

WAGS OF THE BIRD WORLD

Willie Wagtails (*Rhipidura leucophrys*) are quick little flycatchers with a seemingly nervous disposition. They constantly twitter, hop and swivel their tails from side to side. Wagtails belong to the fantail family and use their fanned out wings and tails to help snare passing insects. They also use sheer annoyance as a defence strategy. Knowing that a kookaburra might prey on a Willie Wagtail's small nestlings, they harass the larger bird by continually screeching and trying to push the kookaburra of its perch. This harassment technique often works and the kookaburra flies off to find a more peaceful perch.

The Willie Wagtail's prominent white "eyebrows" are raised in threat when it is defending its territory. Wagtails are courageous little birds, often attacking intruders far larger than themselves.

GRAEME CHAPMAN

Conservation Watch

A rarely seen member of the Dicruridae family is the Yellow-breasted Boatbill (*Machaerirhynchus flaviventer*, left). It occurs in only a small area of rainforest and vine thicket on Cape York Peninsula, Qld.

DUELLING DUETS

Magpie-larks (*Grallina cyanoleuca*) are large terrestrial flycatchers found across most of the Australian mainland. Pairs of Magpie-larks (or Peewees) sing highly coordinated duets to tell other Magpie-larks what a strong relationship they have. Studies have shown that the more coordinated and precise the duet, the more threatened rival birds are and the more they believe the pair-bond is a strong one. Territory is defended by the pair alternating between the male's "peewee" and the female's subsequent "wit" notes. Researchers from the Australian National University recorded both well-timed duets and poorly timed versions and played them back to other Magpie-larks while measuring the rate and strength of replies. They found that birds were far more likely to sing significantly in response to a good duet than to a poor one, indicating that they saw the dynamic duo as more of a threat.

Female Magpie-larks have white chins and a white patch extending down the cheek. Males (above) have black faces with white eyebrows.

the FACTS!

MAGPIE-LARKS are well-known for their habit of attacking window panes, car wheel hubcaps and mirrors. When they see their own reflection they mistake it for an intruder and will attack to defend their territory.

TO CEMENT their nests on tree limbs up to 20 m high, Magpie-larks collect and carry mud in their beaks.

CURIOUSLY, CUCKOO-SHRIKES build tiny nests for their eggs. Once the chicks hatch they quickly become far too big for the nest and have to perch on top of it!

MISTAKEN IDENTITY

Neither cuckoo nor shrike, poor cuckoo-shrikes have long suffered from an undeserved bad reputation. They belong to a family that has about 70 species worldwide. Of the seven species found in Australia, the Black-faced Cuckoo-shrike (*Coracina novaehollandiae*) is the most common. Although they somewhat resemble cuckoos and occasionally steal other birds' nests, they do not impose by laying an egg in a host bird's nest like cuckoos do. The only real resemblance to shrikes, which are not even found in Australia, is the cuckoo-shrike's short, sharp bill, which it uses to grasp and batter insects that it catches in the tree tops. Only the Ground Cuckoo-shrike (*C. maxima*) is terrestrial — all other species enjoy an arboreal lifestyle.

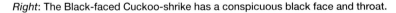

Right: The Black-faced Cuckoo-shrike has a conspicuous black face and throat.

CRASH-LANDING BUG-BASHERS

Cuckoo-shrikes fly with a characteristic undulating (swooping up and down) flight that can make it difficult for them to pursue their swift insect quarry on the wing. To get around this, they employ a novel — although slightly undignified — method of catching food. With wings widespread, they crash-land into the bushy upper foliage of trees, using their wings as feather nets to trap insects.

Cuckoo-shrikes have strong beaks for crushing through an insect's keratinous shell, but the beak is also a useful tool for insect battery! Cuckoo-shrikes regularly bash larger insect prey senseless on a hard surface to break up the shell before consuming their meal.

Sometimes cuckoo-shrikes wait patiently in the branches for insects to pass by; however, they will also try to stir up a meal by ploughing into foliage to shake out insects.

Black & white
Australians

Pied Butcherbird
(*Cracticus nigrogularis*)

Order: Passeriformes
Families: Artamidae & Corvidae

Magpies and butcherbirds are familiar black and white birds in the family Artamidae. These wonderful singers are regularly seen and heard in backyards around the country. Although their raucous cawing is much less welcome in backyards, corvids, which include the jet-black crows, ravens and currawongs, can take comfort in being some of the world's smartest bird species.

the FACTS!

THE NAME BUTCHERBIRD refers to this bird's habit of leaving freshly killed prey wedged in a tree fork in the same way a butcher might let meat hang from a hook.

IN THE 1980s, DNA testing and studies of skull shape proved that woodswallows belonged to the same family (Artamidae) as currawongs, butcherbirds and the Australian Magpie.

RAVENS have a very good sense of smell and can sniff out a rotten carcass from quite a distance.

DESPITE THE CLEVERNESS of crows and ravens (or perhaps because of it!) throughout the ages, they have come to be associated with a darker underworld. In the Middle Ages, people thought they were grave robbers! Even the group nouns used to describe a gathering of some of these species, such as a "murder of crows", a "conspiracy of ravens" and a "tiding of magpies" imply that these birds are somehow sinister.

A ruffle of feathers under the chin distinguishes the Australian Raven from other corvids.

EYE SPY

Although corvids are frequent visitors to parklands and backyards, many species are easily mistaken for another member of the same family. Crows and ravens, especially, are all big glossy black birds that resemble each other closely — only a few telltale factors (such as range and call) determine one species from the other. Adult crows and ravens both have silver-white eyes, but ravens have a ruffle of feathers under the neck. Currawongs are easily identified by their yellow eyes and patches of white plumage. Magpies and butcherbirds can be distinguished by their eye colour — butcherbirds have brown eyes, whereas magpies have red eyes.

SOMETHING TO CROW OVER

Crows, ravens, magpies and the other approximately 120 members of the Corvidae family are some of the brainiest birds in the world. These curious, clever birds have even been observed using tools to help them obtain food. Although they are not predatory birds but voracious scavengers, Australian Ravens (*Corvus coronoides*) have been seen working together to separate a weak lamb from a flock, pecking at its tail until it falls over and is mobbed by its hungry attackers.

BRIGHT-EYED NEST ROBBERS

Three currawong species, which take their name from the Pied Currawong's (below) "carrow, carrow-carrwonk" call, are endemic. Currawongs are characterised by long, sharply pointed beaks with hooked tips, intense yellow eyes and gleaming ebony feathers, although the Grey Currawong (*Strepera versicolor*) can be much paler. They eat just about anything, including fruit, insects, whatever they can scavenge from human garbage cans, and other birds' eggs and nestlings. Currawongs have probably led to the decline of smaller bird species in some regions as their own numbers have increased.

SWOOPING SINGERS

Magpies are talented singers. They can sing notes across four octaves and can also make and memorise hundreds of tunes, as well as remembering at least eight different alarm calls. In many bird species, only males sing, but in magpies both males and females chorus together. A young magpie's song is similar to its parent's song but certain parts are always different. It is thought this may help adults recognise their own grown offspring. The song is almost like a child's name, with parts of the parent's song acting as the "surname" and remaining the same, while the given name is different for each child.

Magpies live in small patriarchal clans in which one dominant male is the ruler of the family. He will eat first and must be obeyed or he pecks at and pulls feathers from the heads of disobedient youngsters. Rolling over is a young magpie's submissive gesture. When they do this, they are saying, "sorry, please don't hurt me".

They are extremely territorial and may engage in aerial combat or border disputes when one clan grows too large for its allotted territory. To do this they may all "walk the line" along their territory, strutting and glaring at a neighbouring clan, or they might fight each other in the air. Many people are fearful of being dive-bombed by broody magpies, but research has shown that magpies only swoop on people they do not recognise. If magpies choose to nest in a backyard or property and regularly see the people who live there while the birds are going about the nest-building process, they will not swoop. However, if a stranger or intruder enters their territory they can become fierce aerial attackers.

the FACTS!

AUSTRALIA'S EARLY SETTLERS thought that if a magpie's tongue was split they could be made to talk. In fact, the tongue has nothing to do with the way magpies sing or mimic humans and thankfully this cruel practice is no longer performed.

PARENT MAGPIES do not discriminate between their chicks but feed them all equally about every twenty minutes (left). They continue to do this for 3–4 months after the chicks have left the nest.

MAGPIE MOTHERS keep the nest clean by removing the eggshell and all the chicks' faeces as part of their daily routine.

PROTECTIVE MAGPIES that nest in parks or near golf courses can give humans a hard peck, but people should remember that the magpies' sole intention is to defend their nest and chicks.

WOODSWALLOWS are the only passerines that do not produce preen oil, instead they have powder-down feathers on the belly. They are also the only songbirds that soar regularly when flying.

WHITE-BREASTED WOODSWALLOWS (*Artamus leucorynchus*) can form flocks of up to 200 birds.

SHARING A ROOST

Of the world's ten woodswallow species, four are uniquely Australian. All species are highly sociable and have a tendency towards group roosting. It has been suggested that they do this to keep warm, but in Australia's sweltering summers this is unlikely. Even in hot weather, groups of woodswallows huddle together on a perch. It may be that when bunched tightly together they appear to be one much larger animal, thus deterring predators.

Below, left to right: Black-faced Woodswallows (*Artamus cinereus*) roosting together on a perch; Little Woodswallows (*Artamus minor*) take opposing views to keep a better lookout.

LEFT: IAN MORRIS

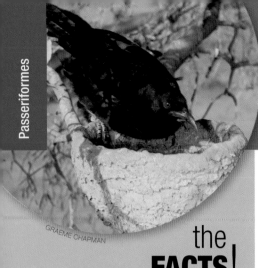

GRAEME CHAPMAN

Mud-nest builders
— choughs & Apostlebirds

Order: Passeriformes
Family: Corcoracidae

Two related Australian species are avian bricklayers that build sturdy nests out of mud and clay. Despite looking little like each other, apart from their dark plumage, the White-winged Chough and the Apostlebird belong to the same family and live similar lifestyles.

the FACTS!

MUD NESTS (above) are built on horizontal branches and are created in several layers, leaving the first layer to dry before adding another. They can take many months to complete and sometimes mud-nesters have to substitute animal dung for mud if mud is scarce.

APOSTLEBIRDS (*Struthidea cinerea*) were thought to live in groups of twelve, hence the name. However they generally form small flocks of 8–20. Sometimes what looks like one bird may be a small group of three or more huddled together (below).

GRAEME CHAPMAN

WHITE-WINGED CHOUGHS are cooperative feeders that forage on the ground and will share with other members of the group if they find a substantial food source.

FLEDGLING White-winged Choughs leave the nest well before they are able to fly, which leaves them highly vulnerable to predation before they reach maturity. Even adults are not strong flyers and prefer to hop from tree limb to tree limb rather than fly.

APOSTLEBIRDS frequently dust-bathe — flapping around in the dirt to remove parasites from feathers.

BOTH THE WHITE-WINGED CHOUGH and the Apostlebird are weak-winged ground-dwelling birds that live in small family groups led by a dominant male with a few females and juveniles in tow.

Although up to three clutches of eggs may be laid in a single season, all hatchlings are slow maturers that may take four years to reach sexual maturity. Until such time, they add to the size of the family flock.

GRAEME CHAPMAN

Adult White-winged Choughs (*Corcorax melanorhamphos*) have red eyes, but when they become excited or alarmed the outer section of the iris becomes engorged and flushes an even brighter red.

BABYSITTERS

Apostlebirds' habitat overlaps with that of the White-winged Chough in some parts of their range. Like choughs they are gregarious and form small family groups (this species is sometimes also referred to as "Happy Families"). Groups flock, forage, preen and build the mud nests cooperatively. During breeding season, which is usually from August to February, more than one female may lay her eggs in the same mud-and-grass nest. Up to eight eggs may be laid, but only four nestlings will survive in the nest's limited space.

GRAEME CHAPMAN

The bowl-sized mud nest of the Apostlebird only has room for four hatchlings. All family members share in raising the young.

Master mimics
— lyrebirds & scrub-birds

Order: Passeriformes
Family: Menuridae & Atrichornithidae

Lyrebirds appear to have no close avian relatives elsewhere in the world and are thought to have evolved on this continent. Behaviourally, they are among the most majestic and interesting bird species.

AUSTRALIA HAS TWO MAGNIFICENT lyrebird species. Albert's Lyrebird (*Menura alberti*) lives only in a small area of forest in New South Wales and Queensland. The Superb Lyrebird (*M. novaehollandiae*) ranges from Victoria along the east coast to southern Queensland.

DANCE FOR ROMANCE

Lyrebirds are best known for their incredible mimicry — they have an extensive repertoire of songs and can mimic chainsaws, dogs and car alarms. Males are also renowned for their long, dazzling tails and impressive dancing. Before dancing, the male must build a suitable dancefloor. He cleans up an area, removing sticks and logs with his feet and scraping together a small mound-like stage. Dancing is a very extravagant affair that includes pulling the tail over the head like a shimmery veil, shaking it and strutting around.

Right, top to bottom: Scratching out a dance platform; A young male shakes his tail feathers.

the FACTS!

SMALL, UNCOMMON SCRUB-BIRDS are unique to Australia and appear to be distantly related to lyrebirds. There are two species, the Rufous Scrub-bird (*Atrichornis rufescens*, above) and the Noisy Scrub-bird (*A. clamosus*). Both are less than 20 cm long and are excellent mimics, uttering loud calls from beneath the understorey of woodland.

LYREBIRDS are the continent's largest songbirds. Both males and females can sing.

ALBERT'S LYREBIRD was named after Queen Victoria's Prince Consort, Prince Albert.

A LYREBIRD kept as a pet by a Victorian flautist learned how to mimic woodwind scales and flute sounds.

MALE LYREBIRDS grow their long outside tail feathers — known as "lyrates" (below), because they are shaped like the curved bow of a lyre — by about six years of age.

LOTHARIO LYRES & SINGLE MUMS

Male lyrebirds are beautiful lotharios. While they perform a magnificent dance and serenade the female with a repertoire of sounds and songs, immediately after mating they move on to another partner. The male's sole desire is mating with as many females as possible during the autumn and winter breeding season. Once he has mated with a female, he is unconcerned with the domesticity of building a nest or raising chicks — he leaves that to the female. A female lyrebird lays just one egg each season and raises her chick as a single mother. First, she builds an incredibly elaborate nest that usually has two chambers — inner and outer — and a roof. The nest can be as much as a metre high and a metre deep and the site is carefully chosen, usually situated between two ferns or in the fork of a tree. The interior is lined with ferns and the mother's own down feathers. As well as being comfortable, the nest must be well hidden because it will be home for the female and her unhatched egg for 50 days until the chick hatches.

MARTIN WILLIS

Show-stoppers
— bowerbirds, catbirds & riflebirds

Order: Passeriformes
Families: Ptilonorhynchidae & Paradisaeidae

Bowerbirds and catbirds belong to the same family, Ptilonorhynchidae, but are not related to the shiny metallic riflebirds, which belong to the Paradisaeidae family. Like the riflebirds, however, they are major show-offs that love to perform to attract females.

the FACTS!

THE MALE Great Bowerbird (*Chlamydera nuchalis*, above) displays a bright pink-purple crest on the nape of his neck when attracting a female.

UNLIKE BOWERBIRDS, catbirds mate for life.

YOUNG MALE Regent Bowerbirds (*Sericulus chrysocephalus*) take up to five years to attain their yellow and black breeding plumage.

FEMALE RIFLEBIRDS sometimes decorate their nests with snakeskin.

YOUNG RIFLEBIRDS may not attain their breeding plumage until they are 3–7 years of age.

THE FEMALE SATIN BOWERBIRD (below) resembles the Spotted Catbird far more than she does her glossy indigo mate.

SATIN BOWERBIRDS that return to their bowers to find them robbed of decorations compensate in a number of ways. To make up for their loss, males will concentrate on improving the paint job of their bower walls (with a mixture of saliva and plant matter) and are also more likely to spend time working on the foundations — gathering more sticks in order to form a more elaborate construction.

M & I MORCOMBE

BOWERBIRDS have a three-fold wooing method. First, construct a bower to be used as a dancefloor in one of four styles — stage bower, avenue bower, maypole bower or mat bower — and decorate it with impressive objects that may include shiny blue objects, moss, white flowers or shells. Second, sing or call to attract a female; and third, when the female approaches, take to the "stage" and strut, head-bob, bow, wing-flap and even throw a few flips if necessary! Females are no less industrious; the bower is not a nest, so the female must build her own saucer-like nest in which to incubate her eggs.

Left: Golden Bowerbirds (*Prionodura newtoniana*) are the smallest bowerbird species but build the largest bowers. Moss and lichen are used to adorn the maypole bower.

BOWER ROBBERS

Male Satin Bowerbirds (*Ptilonorhynchus violaceus*) steal from their neighbours and seem to show a preference for some decorative items over others. Researchers believe that bowerbirds may prefer coloured items that enhance their own colour — so a Satin Bowerbird may prefer blue objects because they accentuate its own shiny blue colour. However, it may also be that particular species are attracted to a given colour because that is their "allotted" colour, which helps species identify each other. Researchers from the University of Queensland discovered that the most prized objects were blue tail feathers from the Crimson Rosella and blue plastic bottle tops.

Satin Bowerbirds build an avenue bower by creating two parallel 50 cm long walls of sticks and stems. The walls of the bower are then "painted" with chewed-up plant matter and the male's saliva.

Conservation Watch

Both the Fawn-breasted and Tooth-billed Bowerbird have limited ranged in far north Queensland, although they are locally common within their range.

THE BEST BOWERS

Males of Australia's eight bowerbird species all look different and each construct bowers with their own species' preferred style of interior design. Bright yellow and black Regent Bowerbirds (right) build an avenue bower decorated with leaves. Shiny Satin Bowerbirds decorate their avenue bower with blue objects. Tooth-billed Bowerbirds (*Scenopoeetes dentirostris*) are the plainest, with speckled plumage, and create an equally simple stage bower by clearing away a platform and piling it with upturned green leaves. Spotted (*Chlamydera maculata*), Western (*C. guttata*) and Great Bowerbirds prefer an twin-walled avenue bower lined with whitened bones, stones and shells and green berries or objects.

CATBIRDS

Australia's two species of noisy catbird are closely related to bowerbirds but do not build bowers. Males and females look alike and both utter a loud "eee-ow" caterwauling noise to get a mate's attention. Catbirds are monogamous and feed on figs, flowers and seeds in subtropical rainforests. They also sometimes visit fruit trees in gardens.

The Green Catbird (*Ailuroedus crassirostris*) is a brilliant emerald green with a spotted underside.

RIFLEBIRDS

Riflebirds are in the same family as the birds of paradise of New Guinea. All four representatives of this family in Australia (including the little known Trumpet Manucode, *Manucodia keraudrenii*) perform elaborate courtship displays. Two species, the Victoria's Riflebird (*Ptiloris victoriae*) and Paradise Riflebird (*P. paradiseus*), are native to Australia. During the breeding season, males face the female, breast to breast, ruffle up their feathers and spread their wings while emitting a raucous rasping noise and raising the head to display their shiny metallic chests.

Left: Male riflebirds make a rasping "yaars" sound and expose the metallic blue chest patch to attract females. *Above, left to right*: While calling, males may also bob their heads up and down and ruffle up their feathers; Males fan out their round-tipped wings and swirl around the female before enfolding her in them and mating.

Specialised
feeders

Order: Passeriformes
Families: Passeridae, Dicaeidae & Nectariniidae

Finches and mannikins are small, colourful birds with short, sharp triangular beaks that are well equipped for crushing hard seed casings. Their spectacular colours and markings have made them popular as pets and aviary birds throughout the world.

the FACTS!

STAR FINCHES (*Neochmia ruficauda*, above) are named for the beautiful spotted "star-like" markings on their chests. Female Star Finches are paler, have less red on their faces and more white spotting on the breast.

AUSTRALIA'S FINCH SPECIES are not true finches, but are actually grassfinches. Two European species introduced to Australia, the Goldfinch (*Carduelis carduelis*) and the Greenfinch (*C. chloris*), are part of the true finch (Fringillidae) family.

HISTORICAL REPORTS suggest that flocks of thousands of Gouldian Finches (*Erythrura gouldiae*) used to wheel across Australia's north; today, there are only about 2000 of these spectacularly coloured finches living in the wild.

THE SOFT CALL of the Double-barred Finch (*Taeniopygia bichenovii*) has been likened to a kitten's mewing.

MISTLETOEBIRDS build a lightweight, suspended nest of vegetation and cobwebs that dangles from a branch or foliage.

Finches, such as the Double-barred Finches above, rarely stray far from freshwater. They drink by sucking up water through their beaks, rather than tipping their heads back to swallow.

FINCHES ARE SPECIALIST seed-eaters, although chicks begin their lives feeding on insects, which contain protein that helps them grow their feathers. All seed-eating birds require a gizzard to help them grind up the tough outer casings and digest the seeds. They also need to drink frequently; as a result, finches are never found far from water. Most live in flocks and males and females form strong pair bonds and cooperate to incubate eggs and raise young.

Right: Gouldian Finches are rare and endangered in the wild but are bred in aviaries around the world. The red-headed form is dominant in captive birds, whereas the black-headed variety is the most common in the wild.

MISTLETOEBIRD

The only Australian representative of the Dicaeidae family of flowerpeckers is the Mistletoebird (*Dicaeum hirundinaceum*). It inhabits most of the continent, apart from Tasmania, and has developed a special relationship with parasitic mistletoes, which grow small red berries that are a crucial part of the Mistletoebird's diet. During the plant's flowering season, nomadic Mistletoebirds move around to make the most of the bounty, swallowing the fruit whole and passing the seed out with their faeces; it then sticks to a tree branch and allows another parasitic plant to grow.

NEST-BUILDING BEAKS

As well as using their beaks to shear seeds, finches and related sparrows use their beaks to help them carry nesting materials such as grasses, twigs and feathers, and to carry objects to "gift" to their mates and partners. Finches build many different types of nests; however, most of them are covered over with a dome shape, leaving just a small, finch-sized entrance. The Blue-faced Parrot-Finch (*Eythrura trichroa*) is a rainforest finch species and its choice of nesting materials includes the tendrils of vines, green moss and grass to help camouflage its nest amid the rainforest greenery. Few species nest in tree hollows, although the Zebra Finch (*Taeniopygia guttata*) and Gouldian Finch have been observed doing so. Because finches' nests are usually deep and dark, all finches lay white eggs, which are easily seen in the darkness.

the FACTS!

RED-EARED FIRETAILS (*Stagonopleura oculata*, below), unlike most grassfinch species, are solitary and do not form flocks.

M & I MORCOMBE

SOMETIMES RED-BROWED FINCHES (*Neochmia temporalis*) form flocks of up to 300 birds, although most flocks number around 30 individuals.

IN ELEVEN of Australia's twenty-odd finch species, males and females appear almost identical.

THE EASTERN RACE of the Star Finch may be extinct in the wild and very few are held in captivity.

A MALE DIAMOND FIRETAIL FINCH (*Stagonopleura guttata*) courts his paramour by offering her a grass stem held in his beak. He then fluffs up his feathers and bobs up and down, by bending his legs, while emitting a buzzing noise.

Some species of finch carry objects, such as feathers or long stems of grass, to their mates.

The Crimson Finch (*Neochmia phaeton*), gets its species name *phaeton* from the son of Helios, the ancient Greek sun-god, because of its glowing sunset colours.

SUNBIRDS

Tiny Yellow-bellied Sunbirds (*Nectarinia jugularis*, left and right) are the only sunbird species in Australia. Sunbirds hover beneath or above nectar-producing flowers and use their long, down-curved beaks to suck up the sugary substance.

Five or six males form a group during breeding season and fly around, chasing each other and trilling loudly. After mating, female sunbirds build suspended, ball-like nests of bark, vegetation and cobwebs with a long, trailing "tail". Unlike finches' eggs, the unrelated sunbird lays beige or buff-coloured eggs.

M & I MORCOMBE

Fruit lovers
— figbirds, orioles & starlings

Order: Passeriformes
Family: Oriolidae & Sturnidae

Two oriole species and the related Figbird inhabit Australia. Starlings are unrelated birds in the family Sturnidae. Although some of them feed primarily on insects, other starling species are common orchard thieves.

the FACTS!

MALE FIGBIRDS (above) can be determined by the bright-red patch of skin around the eye. In contrast, female Figbirds have a blue-grey eye patch.

FIGBIRDS mimic the calls made by other birds, including those of Galahs and Rainbow Lorikeets.

ORIOLES HAVE MELODIOUS, bubbling "ori-ori-ole" calls and are also gifted mimics. Some have been recorded making up to 27 calls.

OLIVE-BACKED ORIOLES (below) are the only birds that Figbirds do not gang up on and chase from their territory. They look very similar to female Figbirds and scientists believe this may be a case of "Batesian mimicry". Batesian mimicry was first observed and named by Henry Walter Bates in the mid-nineteenth century. It refers to one species resembling another (especially a poisonous species) to gain protection.

THE METALLIC STARLING (*Aplonis metallica*) nests in colonies. A cluster of suspended nests, usually of vine tendrils lined with palm leaves, is built in the highest branches of a tree. Each colony can include more than 100 nests.

THE COMMON MYNA (*Acridotheres tristis*) is a starling that was introduced to control insect pests. It is now a major pest because it chases native birds and mammals away from their food source. After land clearing, the Common Myna is the next major threat for some bird species.

Female Figbirds are much more drab than males, but no less noisy.

MARTIN WILLIS

FIGBIRDS (*Sphecotheres viridis*) and oriole species sometimes flock together, but Figbirds can be distinguished by the bare patch of skin around their eyes, which is lacking in oriole species. Rowdy, nomadic flocks of 20–50 birds form to feed on fruiting trees along the continent's eastern and northern coasts and may become even larger in some areas. As their name suggests, Figbirds are especially partial to figs and are helpful seed distributors for Australia's many native fig species.

THE OLIVE-BACKED ORIOLE (*Oriolus sagittatus*) shares a similar range as the Figbird, while the mustard-coloured Yellow Oriole (*O. flavocinctus*) is lesser known and lives only across the Top End from Western Australia to north Queensland.

MICHAEL CERMAK

HEAVY METAL BIRDS

Despite their species name, *metallica*, Metallic Starlings are not named after a heavy metal band, but for their iridescent feathers that have a "metallic" glistening sheen. They are clumsy consumers of fruit and Australia's only native starlings. Metallic Starlings share much of their habitat with the introduced Common Starling (*Sturnus vulgaris*), which is considered a fruit-growers' pest, and the Common Myna, a declared pest.

A colony of Metallic Starlings gathers around the group's communal, bunch-like nests.

Olde-world
relics

Conservation Watch

The rare Zitting Cisticola (*Cisticola juncidis*) has the smallest range of all Sylviidae birds. It is found in only a few regions of north Queensland and the Northern Territory.

Order: Passeriformes
Families: Sylviidae & Zosteropidae

Male Golden-headed Cisticolas (*Cisticola exilis*) perform a fluttering, aerial singing display or carol from a branch during breeding season.

Warblers, grassbirds, songlarks and cisticolas are commonly seen birds of the "old world" — Europe and Asia. Australia has just nine native species out of approximately 339 species worldwide. Although they are known as "old-world warblers", like all passerines their origins are Gondwanan. Australia's native species went on to evolve independently.

HEARD NOT SEEN

Most species in the Sylviidae family are drab, dull-coloured birds that make up for their uninspiring looks with their melodius singing voices. Usually, they can be heard but not seen, although ornithologists and birdwatchers are sometimes able to lure them from their hiding places by making high-pitched sounds or mimicry.

Unlike most other songbirds, native warblers and their relatives are seldom seen in woodlands or forests; most prefer to live among reeds, swamps or tall grasslands, where they are well camouflaged and insects are plentiful. The Spinifexbird (*Eremiornis carteri*) is at home in the arid interior, where it hides among spinifex clumps, and the two uniquely Australian songlarks, the Rufous Songlark (*Cincloramphus mathewsi*) and the Brown Songlark (*C. cruralis*), are also able to withstand the hotter temperatures of the inland. The Rufous Songlark is also one of the few species in this group that frequents timbered country. Some species, such as Tawny Grassbirds (*Megalurus timoriensis*) are seasonal nomads, moving from swamp to swamp.

the FACTS!

SONGLARKS make "song flights" during breeding season, flying above their territory and uttering metallic, squeaking and chattering noises that have led to the Brown Songlark sometimes being known as the "Skit, scot, a-wheeler".

THE LITTLE GRASSBIRD (*Megalurus gramineus*, below) builds a cup-shaped nest that is suspended between the stems of reeds.

CISTICOLAS conceal their nests by using cobwebs to "sew" green leaves to the outside.

THE MALE BROWN SONGLARK (below) is much larger and darker in colour than his mate. Males can grow to 25 cm while the female is usually only about 18–19 cm long.

ASIAN IMMIGRANTS

White-eyes (Australia has six species) and the Silvereye, belong to the Zosteropidae family and have all spread to Australia from Asia. Around the world there are as many as 80 species. They are identifiable by the white (or silver) ring around their eyes, but distinctions between the species are less obvious. Aphids, insects and fruit comprise most of their diet, although they also have brush-tipped tongues for eating nectar.

The Silvereye (*Zosterops lateralis*) inhabits most of the southern and eastern coasts.

Conservation Watch

The Red-lored Whistler is considered vulnerable due to its tiny range. The Golden Whistler (*Pachycephala pectoralis*) is also vulnerable on Norfolk Island.

Loud & proud
— a symphony of songsters

Order: Passeriformes
Families: Pachycephalidae, Pomatostomidae, Meliphagidae & Orthonychidae

As their names imply, whistlers, bellbirds and shrike-thrushes are all singing sensations that perform a variety of ear-pleasing tunes. Babblers, in the family Pomatosomidae, are just that — sociable and bubbly songbirds that "babble" in noisy chatter. Logrunners and chowchillas may have more obscure common names, but they too have powerful voices.

APART FROM THE CRESTED BELLBIRD (*Oreoica gutturalis*) and three shrike-tit species, Australia is inhabited by eight whistler and four shrike-thrush species. Whistlers sing long, loud whistling songs, while shrike-thrushes have shorter, more complex tunes. Logrunners (*Orthonyx temminicki*) and the Chowchilla (*O. spaldingii*) are ground-dwelling, rainforest birds that rarely fly, preferring to peck for insects in the leaf litter. They create a nest of vine tendrils in the buttress of a tree root.

the FACTS!

THE EASTERN SHRIKE-TIT (above) has a chirruping call that has been likened to singing "knock at the door".

TO GET A BETTER VIEW of possible victims in the leaf litter, the Chowchilla (below) uses an uncommon side-kicking action to scrape away leaves on the rainforest floor.

HALL'S BABBLER (*Pomatostomus halli*) was only discovered in 1964; before then it was confused with the White-browed Babbler (*P. superciliosus*).

THE CRESTED BELLBIRD was called *panpanpanella* by Aborigines, in imitation of the cadence of its ringing call. Early European settlers called the bird "dick-dick-the-devil".

LOGRUNNERS (right) have a fossil record that dates back about 15 million years.

Above, left to right: Grey-crowned Babblers (*Pomatostomus temporalis*) are the largest of their kind; The Red-lored Whistler (*Pachycephala rufogularis*) occupies an extremely restricted range.

BIRDS WITH BELLS

Bell Miners' tinkling bell-like calls are often heard well before the birds are seen because their grey-green plumage allows them to blend in with their woodland habitat. They are honey-eaters that have brush-tipped tongues for soaking up sugary nectar, but a major part of their diet is lerps, or the sweet casing of psyllid larvae. To protect their food source, bellbirds form colonies of up to 200 birds and use "gang warfare" to chase larger birds out of their territory. This sometimes has disastrous results for the trees, as the Bell Miners "harvest" the bugs but do not eat them all.

Right: Many people know the Bell Miner as the Bellbird.

Hunters
on the wing

Orders: Passeriformes & Apodiformes
Families: Hirundinidae & Apodidae

Slim, streamlined bodies and long, tapered wings give swallows, swifts and martins an aerial advantage over their insect prey. Swallows and martins look alike and are both quick little hunters — the easiest way to tell them apart is by their tails. A swallow's tail is forked; a martin's is short and square. Swifts belong to a different order altogether.

Above: Small Fairy Martins (*Hirundo ariel*) are migratory birds that fly north in winter, sometimes even flying to New Guinea.

SWALLOWS AND MARTINS do almost everything on the wing. Insects are snatched up in mid-air and water is scooped up "on the fly" when the birds skim over rivers or lakes. Even a bath is largely an aerial affair, with the birds simply swooping down to the water's surface to wet their wings, and then flapping them clean.

The Swallow family is well-known and widespread, with 74 worldwide species. Four are native to Australia, but only one — the White-backed Swallow (*Cheramoeca leucosternus*) — is unique to Australia. All of them are highly mobile and either migrate northwards just before cold weather sets in or are entirely nomadic.

NAMED FOR SPEED

Swifts and swiftlets are, as their names suggest, fast-flying insect-catchers; however, they belong to a different order to swallows and martins. Swifts, swiftlets and needletails belong to the Apodiformes order. Because they spend so much time flying, their legs and feet are weak, unlike those of the perching passerine swallows and martins. All except the White-rumped Swiftlet are migrants.

CAVE DWELLERS

A feature that swiftlets share with some swallows is a preference for dark nest sites. White-backed Swallows dig long, dark tunnels for their nests. Nesting tunnels can be up to a metre long with an open chamber at the end, where a cup-shaped depression is dug out. Welcome Swallows (*Hirundo neoxena*) sometimes create their cup-shaped nests in cliffs and overhangs, or nest in small caves. White-rumped Swiftlets (*Collocalia spodiopygius*, right) nest and roost in dark caves and crevices.

GRAHAM ANDERSON/ANT PHOTO

the FACTS!

WELCOME SWALLOWS (above) serenade females on the wing during breeding.

TREE MARTINS (*Hirundo nigricans*, below) are the only native species in this family that nests in trees.

FAIRY MARTINS (*Hirundo ariel*) are mud-nesters that breed in colonies and construct bottle-shaped nests under overhangs, bridges, culverts and in cliffs. Some colonies are made up clusters of hundreds of mud-nests.

THE LARGEST SWALLOW to be found in Australia is the Red-rumped Swallow (*Hirundo daurica*), which is a rare migrant from Asia.

SWIFTLETS use echolocation to navigate in dark caves in a similar way that bats do. They emit clicking sounds and listen for the direction of echoes.

Conservation
— an uncertain future

Our lifestyles impact on birds in many ways and often degrade their habitat. This fact, coupled with natural deaths by predation and competition, could spell disaster for some bird species. Because many birds are migratory, protecting them is everyone's responsibility and must be a matter of global importance.

the FACTS!

BIRDS FREQUENTLY FLY into house, school and office windows as well as into moving cars. Roads and cars are not only taking lives, they may also be altering the breeding success of some bird species by muffling the bird's song. International studies have shown that some birds with lower pitched calls cannot be heard over traffic noise when they live close to developed areas and have had to alter their songs to a higher pitched tune. If a bird's mate cannot hear it call, this could affect the species' breeding rate.

THE BIRD TRADE dramatically decreased numbers of some birds.

CHEMICAL POLLUTION and oil spills can wipe out many thousands of seabirds. In 1989, the *Exxon Valdez* oil spill in Alaska was estimated to have killed 500,000 birds in a matter of days. As well as poisoning birds and making them waterlogged, oil destroys mangroves, coral reefs and marine vegetation. Detergent used in an effort to wash and save birds also often stripped the waterproofing from feathers. In 2004, researchers from Victoria University developed an environmentally friendly way to help oil-sodden birds in the form of an iron powder spray that soaks up oil on birds' feathers and can then be stripped away using magnets.

IN THE EARLY DAYS of European settlement in Australia, most people were unaware or unconcerned about how human activities could affect birds. Vast tracts of bushland were cleared to build towns and farms. Rivers and creeks were dammed and used for irrigation. Many species of waterfowl and pigeon were hunted as food, and beautiful parrots and wild birds were trapped and sold as cage birds. Even birds' eggs made their way onto the dinner plates of settlers. The bird trade of the nineteenth and early twentieth centuries was responsible for the deaths of many millions of birds for their feathers (as in the case of egrets), meat and skins.

TODAY, Australia's native bird species are protected and many of the former threats, such as hunting, have been removed. Despite these measures, birds still remain at risk from habitat destruction, competition with introduced bird species, predation by introduced foxes, cats and dogs, poisoning of their prey and illegal trapping and smuggling.

A GLOBAL ISSUE

Like many animal species, birds act as an early-warning system for environmental disaster. When bird species start to decline in any one place, it indicates that other environments and ecosystems are also likely to come under threat or be affected. For migratory birds, global networks, conventions and agreements aim to protect areas of critical importance and monitor bird populations in countries around the world. However, many more vital areas that birds use as permanent or transitory habitats also require protection.

Above and left: Cats were introduced to Australia on the First Fleet. Today, feral cats decimate bird populations and have contributed to the extinction of many species.

LEFT: GARY STEER; ABOVE: GC QM

Saving
Australia's birds

Saving threatened species depends first on understanding them and their role in the ecosystems in which they live. Only then can we take measures to preserve their lifestyles and protect them for future generations.

WHAT YOU CAN DO

Learning more about birds is the first vital step in helping to protect them. Preserving their habitat is the second. Planting native species in your garden means you not only use less water, you also provide an important food source for birds. You can also hang artificial nesting hollows in your garden to create nesting spaces. To help keep our rivers and oceans clean for the birds and animals that live there, you should be careful to use environmentally friendly detergent products and fertilisers. Above all, one of the most important things you can do is be vocal — lend your support to conservation societies and national parks and wildlife services.

Birds such as the Yellow-tufted Honeyeater (*Lichenostomus melanops*) depend upon flowering native species for food.

the FACTS!

THE ORANGE-BELLIED PARROT (above) is critically endangered.

EACH YEAR, more than 300,000 seabirds, including pelicans and albatrosses, drown because they are accidentally caught on baited hooks.

IN LATE 2006, the World Wildlife Fund released a report (*Bird Species and Climate Change: The Global Status Report*) that estimated that as many as 72% of north-eastern Australian bird species could vanish if global warming raises the planet's temperature by as little as 2°C.

CHRISTMAS ISLAND has been listed by Birdlife International as a "key bird endemicity area". Ten bird species on the island are critically endangered, including the Christmas Island White-eye, the Brown Goshawk, the Emerald Dove, and one of most endangered avian species in the world, Abbott's Booby.

BIRDSTRIKES occur when birds collide with planes or the rotors of helicopters. A 2003 study suggested that birdstrikes are increasing considerably. Between 1991 and 2001, Australia reported 3310 instances of birdstrike, mostly involving hawks, galahs, gulls, magpies, eagles and ibises.

SAVING HABITAT

Land clearing for agriculture and urban development poses one of the biggest threats to Australia's native species. The first *Australian Terrestrial Biodiversity Assessment* report, conducted in 2002, suggested that 2891 separate Australian ecosystems were at risk due to land clearing and habitat destruction. Out of the 384 regions examined during the eighteen-month study, native birds were at risk in 240 regions! Since then, global warming has only added to this diagnosis. Birds are a crucial part of our worldwide ecosystems. They help keep insect populations under control and many plants rely on them for pollination. Birds that have a co-dependent relationship with certain plant species suffer if those trees are removed from their environment. Habitat destruction does not just rob birds of their home territories, it can also ruin their nest sites and hollows, and pollute or destroy their food and water sources. State and federal governments are working together to limit land clearing and degradation and better manage vegetation throughout the continent.

The endangered Golden-shouldered Parrot (*Psephotus chrysopterygius*).

Glossary

ALTRICIAL (YOUNG) Chicks that cannot move about independently or feed themselves for some time after hatching.

ARBOREAL Living in trees.

AVIAN Relating to birds.

BINOCULAR (VISION) Physiological adaptation whereby each eye is used together. Allows for depth perception and the accurate judging of distances. Typical of predators such as hawks, eagles etc.

BROOD To sit on and keep eggs warm. To incubate.

CLOACA Final section of the gut in birds, reptiles and amphibians. Faeces, urine and reproductive cells pass out of the cloaca in most birds. (Male ducks, Emus and cassowaries transfer semen through an organ extruded from the cloaca).

COVERTS Small feathers that cover the bases of other larger feathers.

DISPLAY Behaviour used to communicate with other birds using plumage, movement, voice and objects (e.g. food or nesting material).

ECHOLOCATION Sensing objects by perceiving sound waves reflected from them. Used by a few bird species.

ENDEMIC Found in a particular location and nowhere else.

EVERT To turn inside out.

EYRIE A high nest used by birds of prey.

FERAL A domestic animal (e.g. cat) that has become wild.

GENUS A group of one or more closely related species of animals/plants. The first Latin name of an animal's/plant's scientific name is the genus. Different species can share the same genus.

HATCHLING Young bird that has recently broken free from its egg.

IUCN RED LIST List describing the conservation status of threatened species published by the International Union for the Conservation of Nature and Natural Resources.

KERATINOUS Relating to keratin — a tough protein that forms hard body parts (e.g. nails, shells etc.) in many animals.

LERP Sugary secretion produced by psyllids (a group of small, plant-eating insects).

LORE Space between the eyes and the base of the bill.

MEGAPODE Mound-building bird.

MIGRATION Seasonal movement from one area to another. May take place within Australia or to and from other countries.

MIMIC To copy vocally, especially the sounds made by other bird species.

MONOCULAR (VISION) Physiological adaptation whereby each eye is used separately. Increases field of view.

MOULT Process of shedding and replacing feathers.

NECTARIVORE An animal that feeds on the nectar of flowering plants.

NOMAD An animal that moves from place to place.

PASSERINE Order of birds in which species have three toes directed forward and one backward. A well-developed voice box (syrinx) allows passerine species to form complex songs.

PELLET Package of indigestible material regurgitated by owls etc.

PLUMAGE A bird's feathers.

POLYGAMY A reproductive strategy whereby one male mates with a number of females.

POLYANDRY A reproductive strategy whereby one female mates with a number of males.

PRECOCIAL (YOUNG) Chicks that are able to leave the nest soon after hatching.

PREEN To arrange feathers by "zipping up" barbs and dressing them with oil from preen gland.

RAPTOR A diurnal bird of prey.

RATITE Large, flightless bird (many of which are now extinct).

SYRINX A bird's voice box. Situated at the lower end of the trachea (windpipe). Particularly well developed in passerines.

TERRESTRIAL Living on land.

VIBRISSAE Special feathers located near the mouths of some birds.

ZYGODACTYLUS Having two pairs of toes on each foot — one forward-facing pair and one backward-facing pair.

PUBLICATIONS:

Beruldsen, G. *Australian Birds: Their Nests and Eggs*, G & E Beruldsen, Kenmore Hills, Qld, 2004

Burnie, D. *Birds: Collins Eyewitness Guide*, HarperCollins, Auckland, NZ, 1996

Bransbury, J. *Where to Find Birds in Australia*, Waymark Publishing Australia, Fulllarton, SA, 1992

Cooke, Dingle & Hutchinson, McKay, *The Encyclopedia of Animals: A Complete Visual Guide*, University of California Press, LA, 2004

Currey, K. *Fact File Birds*, Steve Parish Publishing, Brisbane, 2006

Debus, S. *The Birds of Prey of Australia*, Oxford University Press, 1998

Egerton, L. (Ed.), *Encyclopedia of Australian Wildlife*, Reader's Digest, Sydney, 2005

Egerton, L. *Know Your Birds: Australia's Most Common Birds*, Reed New Holland, Sydney, 2004

Forshaw, J. (Ed.), *Encyclopedia of Birds*, University of Sydney Press, Weldon Owen, 1998

Ganeri, A. *Focus on the Living World: Birds*, Aladdin Books Ltd, London, 2003

Johnstone, R.E. & Storr, G.M. *Handbook of Western Australian Birds, Vol 1: Non-passerines (Emu to Dollarbird)*, Western Australian Museum, 1998

Johnstone, R.E. et al. *Handbook of Western Australian Birds, Vol 2: Passerines (Blue-winged Pitta to Goldfinch)*, Western Australian Museum, 2004

Kaplan, G. *Famous Australian Birds*, Allen & Unwin, NSW, 2003

Lindsey, T. *Green Guide: Parrots of Australia*, New Holland Publishers, Sydney, 1998

McNaughton, M. *Australian Parrots and Finches*, Bluestone Press, Vic, 2004

Mobbs, A.J. *The Complete Book of Australian Finches*, T.F.H. Publications, New Jersey, USA, 1990

Morcombe, M. *Field Guide to Australian Birds*, Steve Parish Publishing, Brisbane, 2003

Pizzey, G. & Knight, F. *Field Guide to the Birds of Australia*, HarperCollins, Sydney, 1997

Rabinowitz, S. *Parrots*, Creative Education, Minnesota, 2002

Slater, P. *Amazing Facts About Australian Birds*, Steve Parish Publishing, Brisbane, 1999

Taylor, B. *DK Pockets: Birds*, Dorling Kindersley, London, 1995

Trounson, D. & M. *Australian Birds: Simply Classified* (4th ed.) Murray David Publishing Pty Ltd, Frenchs Forrest, NSW, 1998

WEBSITES:

www.newscientist.com

www.newsinscience.com

www.birdsaustralia.com.au

www.ausraptor.org.au

www.ausbird.com

www.absa.asn.au

www.iucnredlist.org

www.anbg.gov.au/birds/birds.html

www.austmus.gov.au/birds/stuff/bird_list.htm

Index